TO
OLLAM

75p

DIGITALLY REPRODUCED

2005

"CPC has carried out research on current Copyrights to no avail"

AVAILABLE AT:

COVENANT BOOKS
121 Low Etherley
Bishop Auckland
Co. Durham
DL14 0HA

DISCOVERY

OF THE TOMB OF

(Olläv Fóla),

IRELAND'S FAMOUS MONARCH AND LAW-MAKER UPWARDS
OF THREE THOUSAND YEARS AGO.

BY

EUGENE ALFRED CONWELL,

M.R.I.A., M.A.I., F.R. HIST. SOC., &c.,

INSPECTOR OF IRISH NATIONAL SCHOOLS.

"That speechless past has begun to speak."—PALGRAVE.

With Fifty-six Illustrations.

DUBLIN:

McGLASHAN & GILL, 50, UPPER SACKVILLE-STREET.

LONDON: WILLIAMS & NORGATE, HENRIETTA-ST., COVENT GARDEN.

EDINBURGH: EDMONSTON & DOUGLAS, PRINCE'S-ST.

1873.

Printed and bound
by Antony Rowe Ltd, Eastbourne

PREFACE.

SOME portions of the following pages were originally contributed to the Proceedings of the Royal Irish Academy,* in a Paper read at a meeting of that body on 12th February, 1872, "On the Identification of the Ancient Cemetery at Loughcrew, Co. Meath, and the Discovery of the Tomb of Ollamh Fodhla."

Our attempt to rescue from the domain of legend and romance the memories of a locality, at one time the most famous in our island, and in so doing to revive a faded and long forgotten page in early Irish History, is here presented to our fellow-countrymen, in the hope that it may be found not only not uninteresting to them, but that it may be the means of inducing others, in various localities, to turn their attention to, and to elucidate whatever remains of Ireland's Ancient Relics may be still extant in their respective vicinities.

Our very grateful thanks are pre-eminently due to the late J. L. W. Naper, Esq., D. L., who, from the time we commenced our antiquarian researches on the Loughcrew Hills, in 1863, uniformly encouraged and aided us in supplying the amount of manual labour necessary for carrying on the explorations, without which friendly encouragement and patriotic help, whilst others laughed at what appeared to them the foolish and childish occupation of a "visionary antiquary" turning over old stones, no practical result would probably ever have been arrived at. Had he lived to see it shown that the greatest, the oldest, and the most important of the Ancient Royal Pagan Cemeteries of Ireland existed on and around his own hills, we can only imagine the amount of self-satisfaction with which he would have looked back upon the part he took in contributing to restore the historic memories of the place.

---

* See Vol. I., Ser. II., Pol. Lit. and Antiq., page 72, &c.

No less deeply grateful can we feel for the steps taken by his agent, Charles William Hamilton, Esq., J. P., Hamwood, well known to be ever ready to lend a helping hand to scientific progress. He not only from the first enthusiastically entered into our views by being practically present, and by taking an active part in all the operations; but, when we pointed out that the carns at Loughcrew were not recorded on the Ordnance Maps, he at once communicated with Major-General Sir Henry James, R. E., F. R. S., Director of the Ordnance Survey, calling his attention to the omission, and with praiseworthy alacrity a highly accomplished Sapper, Mr. Thomas Pearson, was sent from the Ordnance Department, Phœnix Park, with instructions to resurvey the hills, and to insert the antiquities, while our examination of them was in progress, in September, 1865, on a map 25·344 inches to a statute mile. This map, under the title of "Plan of the Sepulchral Carns of Loughcrew, in the county of Meath" (sheets 9 and 15, Part I. and Part II.), was afterwards zincographed in 1868, at the Ordnance Survey Office, Phœnix Park, under the direction of Captain Wilkinson, R. E.; and copies of it, in two parts, can be obtained from Hodges, Foster, and Co., 104, Grafton-street, Dublin.

It will be gratifying intelligence to all those who have the preservation of archæological remains at heart to know, that the present proprietor of Loughcrew, J. L. Naper, Esq., D. L., has intimated to us, since the following pages were printed, his intention of having all necessary steps taken for the due care and preservation of the highly interesting remnants of antiquity on his property.

In the hope that it may be found useful we give a brief account of the ancient Irish MSS. we have used as authorities, and without calling in the aid of which we never could have attempted to restore the long-forgotten name and history of the Cemetery on the Loughcrew Hills. It is admitted by all who have studied the subject that the early history of Ireland never can be written until all the ancient Irish MSS. still extant are made accessible to the general reader: and this only can be done by multiplying copies and translating them. Acting on this enlightened view the Librarian of the Royal Irish Academy, John T. Gilbert, Esq., F. S. A., as a member of their council, submitted, in 1869, a suggestion for the publication of ancient Irish texts in their original integrity. The first result of the adoption of this suggestion was the publication in November, 1870, of two hundred copies from the original in the Library of the Royal Irish Academy, of LEABHAR NA H-UIDHRI; with an account of the manuscript itself, a description of its contents, an index, and *fac-similes* in colours. This MS., the oldest volume now known entirely in the Irish language, is regarded as the chief surviving native literary monument, not ecclesiastical, of ancient Ireland. We submit a condensed notice of it from O'Curry's "Lectures on the Manuscript Materials of Ancient Irish History," p. 182, &c. :—

" The first of these ancient books that merits notice, because it is the oldest, is that which is known by the name of LEABHAR NA H-UIDHRI, or the Book of the Dun Cow :—said to have been so called from the fact of St. Ciaran having written down in a book, which he had made from the hide of his pet cow, one of the principal tracts contained in LEABHAR NA H-UIDHRI, viz., the celebrated tale of the *Táin Bó Chuailgne*, or ' Plunder of the Cows of Cuailgne' (a district now called Cooley, in the county of Louth, stretching along the bay of Carlingford). This cow from its colour was called *Odhar*, or dark grey, or dun ; and the form *Uidhri* being the genitive case of the word *Odhar*, the book was ever afterwards known, from this circumstance, as *Leabhar na h-Uidhri*, or ' Book of the dun (cow).' See ' O'Curry's Lectures,' page 30.

" Of the original compiler and writer of *Leabhar na h-Uidhri*, I have been able to learn nothing more than a brief and melancholy notice of his death in the Annals of the Four Masters, at the year 1106. A memorandum in the original hand, at the top of folio 45, clearly identifies the writer of the book with the person whose death is recorded in the passage in the Annals.

" The contents of the MS., as they stand now, are of a mixed character, historical and romantic, and relate to the ante-Christian, as well as the Christian period. The book begins with a fragment of the Book of Genesis, part of which was always prefixed to the Book of Invasions (or ancient Colo- nization) of Erinn, for genealogical purposes.

" This is followed by a fragment of the history of the Britons, by Nennius, translated into Gaedhlic by *Gilla Caomhain*, the poet and chronologist, who died A. D. 1072.

" The next important piece is the very ancient elegy, written by the poet *Dallan Forgaill*, on the death of Saint Colum Cille, in the year 592.

" The elegy is followed by fragments of the ancient historic tale of the *Mesca Uladh*, [or Inebriety of the Ultonians,] who in a fit of excitement after a great feast at the royal palace of Emania, made a sudden and furious march into Munster, where they burned the palace of *Teamhair Luachra*, in Kerry, then the residence of *Curoi Mac Daire*, king of West Munster. This tract abounds in curious notices in topography, as well as in allusions to and descriptions of social habits and manners.

" Next come fragments of *Táin Bó Dóartadha*, and the *Táin Bó Flidais ;* both Cattle Spoils, arising out of the celebrated Cattle Spoil of *Cuailnge*. Next comes the story of the wanderings of Maeldun's ship in the Atlantic, for three years and seven months, in the eighth century. These are followed by imperfect copies of: the *Táin Bó Chuailgne*, or great Cattle Spoil of *Cuailgne ;* the *Bruighean Da Dearga*, and death of the monarch *Conaire Mór ;* a history of the great pagan cemeteries of Erinn, and of the various old books from which this and other pieces were compiled ; poems by Flann of Monasterboice and others; together with various other pieces of history and historic romance, chiefly referring to the ante-Christian period, and especially that of the *Tuatha Dé Danann.* This most valuable MS. belongs to the Royal Irish Academy."

The same authority* gives us the following account of LEABHAR LECAIN, or the Book of Lecan, so styled from the name of the place (Lecan), at which it was compiled.

" This Book was compiled in the year 1416, by *Gilla Isa Mór* Mac Firbis, of *Lecan Mic Fhirbisigh,* in the county of Sligo, one of the great school of teachers of that celebrated locality, and the direct ancestor of the learned *Dubhaltach* [or Duald] Mac Firbis. This Book, which belongs to the Library of the Royal Irish Academy, contains over 600 pages, equal to 2400 pages of the Gaedhlic text of the ' Annals of the Four Masters.' It is beautifully and accurately written on vellum of small folio size, chiefly in the hand of *Gilla Isa* Mac Firbis, though there are some small parts of it written, respectively, in the hands of Adam *O'Cuirnin* (the historian of *Breifñe,* or Briefney) and Morogh *Riabhac O'Cuindlis.* And here I may perhaps be permitted to observe, that I believe the families of Forbes and Candlish in Scotland are the same as, and indeed directly descended from, those of Mac Firbis and O'Cuindlis in Ireland.

" The first nine folios of the Book of Lecan were lost, until discovered by me a few years ago, bound up in a volume of the Seabright Collection, in the Library of Trinity College.

" The Book of Lecan differs but little, in its arrangement and general con-tents, from the Book of Ballymote. It contains two copies of the Book of Invasions, an imperfect one at the beginning, but a perfect one, with the Suc-cession of the Kings, and the tract on the Boromean Tribute, at the end. It contains fine copies of the ancient historical, synchronological, chronological, and genealogical poems already spoken of as comprised in the Book of Bally-mote, as well as some that are not contained in that volume. These are followed by the family history and genealogies of the Milesians, with con-siderable and important additions to those found in the Book of Ballymote. Among the additions is a very valuable tract, in prose and verse, by Mac Firbis himself, on the families and sub-divisions of the territory of *Fir-Fi-achrach,* in the present county of Sligo ; a tract which has been published by the Irish Archæological Society, under the title of ' The Tribes and Customs of Hy-Fiachrach.' "

We have to acknowledge our obligations to Brian O'Looney, Esq., M. R. I. A., successor in the Chair of Celtic Literature to the late eminent Eugene O'Curry, for his valuable assistance in collating and revising the Irish texts quoted in the succeed-ing pages. To him, also, we are indebted for the following ex-

* "O'Curry's Lectures on the Manuscript Materials of Ancient Irish History," p. 192.

planation of the word DINDSENCHAS,* the name of a celebrated
ancient topographical tract giving the history of the *eminent,
distinguished,* or *notable* places in Erin, and said to be compiled at
Tara about the year 550.†

"*Dindsenchas* literally means 'History of the Eminences;' but there are
many different pieces under this title which should not be confounded, e. g.,
the tract from which I gave you the extract on the 'Fair of Tailtiu,' is,
called '*Dindsenchas Erion,*' or the 'History of the Eminent Places in Erin.'
Again we have '*Dindsenchas Dindna Erion,*' the 'History of the eminent
fastnesses and fortified places in Erin;' and another tract called '*Dindsenchas na Curad,*' the 'History of the eminent Warriors and Champions of
Erin;' and several other pieces of this nature which, though totally distinct, are collectively called *Dindsenchas.*"

THE ANNALS OF IRELAND to which, as will be seen, we have so
often referred, were called by Colgan, the friend and cotemporary
of Michael O'Clery, *Annales Quatuor Magistrorum,* and also *Annales Dungallenses,* the latter name being applied from the fact of
their having been commenced and compiled at the Franciscan
Convent of *Donegal.* The title of *Four Masters* was never assumed
by the compilers themselves. Colgan, in his preface to his *Acta
Sanctorum Hiberniæ,* gives his reasons for so denominating them;
and Dr. O'Donovan remarks that as *Quatuor Magistri* had been
long previously applied by the medical writers of the middle
ages to the Four Masters of the Medical Sciences, this circumstance may probably have suggested to Colgan the appellation
he has given to the compilers of these Annals, which, in themselves, we think, should never have been known by any other
name than the simple one of the *Annals of Donegal.* The four
principal scribes, however, employed in compiling them, having
been four most eminent masters in antiquarian lore, at the
period in which they flourished, may have in no small degree
contributed to their work being now so favourably and so
popularly known as the ANNALS OF THE FOUR MASTERS. Their
names were Michael, Conary, and Cucogry O'Clery, together
with Ferfeasa O'Mulconry.

1. Michael O'Clery, the chief of the Four Masters, was born
in the parish of Kilbarron, near Ballyshannon, about the year
1580, and was descended from a family of hereditary scholars.
He is said to have received, if not his classical, at least his

* Pronounced *Dinshanahus.*
† "O'Curry's Lectures," p. 188.

Gaedhlic education, in the south of Ireland, from *Baothghalach Ruadh** Mac Ægan. After a most laborious career as a scribe and compiler from ancient records then in existence, he closed, according to Harris, his useful life in 1643.

2. Conary O'Clery, the second Annalist, was not a member of any religious order. Without having any property, except his learning, he appears to have acted as scribe, and, in such capacity, to have transcribed the greater portion of the Annals, probably at the dictation of his brother, or under his directions, from other manuscripts. His descendants, if he left any, are unknown.

3. Cucogry or Peregrine O'Clery was the head of the Tyrconnell sept of the O'Clerys. In addition to various other contributions to Irish literature, he wrote in Irish a life of the celebrated Hugh Roe O'Donnell, who died in Spain in 1602. Having removed to Ballycroy, in the south of the barony of Erris, in the county of Mayo, he died there in 1664, leaving by his will his books, which were his chief treasure, to his two sons, Dermot and John.

4. Nothing is known of the fourth Master, Ferfeasa O'Mulconry, except that he was a native of the county of Roscommon and a hereditary antiquary.

The compilation of *The Annals of Ireland* by these four scribes consisted in digesting and transcribing the records (most of the originals of which have been since lost), which had descended to them : and a minute and highly interesting account of these labours, and of the old books and authorities made available on the occasion, will be found in Dr. O'Donovan's "Introductory Remarks" to his elaborate translation of their work, as well as in Professor O'Curry's "Lectures on the Manuscript Materials of Ancient Irish History," p. 140 to p. 162. The Work having been drawn up in two parts, when completed, was dedicated by "Brother Michael O'Clery" to *Fearghal O'Gadhra* (Fergal or Ferall O'Gara), hereditary Lord of *Magh Ui Gadhra* (Moy O'Gara) and *Cuil O-bh-Finn* (Coolavin) in the county of Sligo. From this dedication we learn that the compilation was undertaken at the suggestion and cost of the said Ferall O'Gara, "Prince of Coolavin," and the patron of Michael O'Clery.

The last sentence in the dedication states :—"On the 22nd January, 1632, this work was undertaken in the convent of Dun-na-ngall, and was finished in the same convent on 10th of

---

* Pronounced *Baoghla Roe*, or *Bayla Rue*.

August, 1636." This, though substantially, cannot be literally correct ; for the convent was a ruin for upwards of thirty years before the work was commenced. At a short distance from the town of Donegal the remains of the monastery are still to be seen. It was founded in 1474 by Hugh Roe, son of Niall Garbh O'Donnell, Chief of Tyrconnell, and his wife, Finola, daughter of Conor na Srona O'Brien, king of Thomond. On 2nd of August, 1601, it was occupied by a garrison of 500 English soldiers. Shortly after O'Donnell laid siege to this garrison. On the 19th of September following the building took fire ; and, with the exception of one corner, was completely destroyed. After the restoration of Rory O'Donnell, the brotherhood were permitted to return and live in cottages near the monastery ; and it must have been in one of these cottages that the work was compiled.

It has not been accurately determined at what period the practice of recording public events in the shape of Annals commenced in Ireland. We have, however, a very remarkable proof of the general trustworthiness and accuracy of the old records (many of which, now lost, were transcribed into MSS. we still possess), in the precision with which the compilers of the Annals of Tighernach and Ulster have transmitted the account of an eclipse of the sun, which took place A. D. 664. Venerable Bede, who is followed by the Four Masters, mentions the solar eclipse as having occurred on the 3rd day of May, having evidently calculated the time according to the Dionysian cycle, the error of which had not been detected in his time ; while the Annals of Tighernach and Ulster have preserved the exact day and hour (1st of May, about 10 o'clock), having copied the entry from the record of some eye-witness, who, without any necessary acquaintance with the laws of Astronomy, had simply seen the eclipse, and noted it at the time of observation.[*]

We would fail in our duty if we did not here record the great care with which our artist, Herr Wilhelm Tomsohn, of the printing house of Forster and Co., Dublin, during the month of July, 1867, under our own eye and correction, drew the various devices on the inscribed stones in the different carns ; and the fidelity with which these, in the one we here presume to designate the Tomb of Ollamh Fodhla, have been en-

---

[*] See Dr. O'Donovan's Introductory Remarks to Four Masters, page xlviii., and vol. i. p. 277, note x.

b

graved by Mr. C. D. Cooper, Strand, London.   The chief illustrations at pages 25, 28, 30, 33, 39, and 62 have been most
artistically rendered by Mr. R. B. Utting, 33, Camden-road,
London ; and those at pages 2, 4, 22, 53, 54, 55, 56, 57, and 61,
have been engraved by Mr. William Oldham, Dublin.

   TRIM, 1*st August*, 1873.

DISCOVERY

OF THE

TOMB OF OLLAMH FODHLA.

IN all Ireland there is probably no other locality which contains, associated together in such close proximity, so many still existing landmarks, literally speaking, of the social, political, and religious condition of the inhabitants of the country in pre-Christian times, as the neighbourhood of the town of Oldcastle, in the county of Meath, presents for the study of the archæologist; and yet, strange to say, this most historic district has hitherto escaped the observation and inquiry which the memories of such objects have usually attracted, their histories in a great measure having only descended to us through the philological meanings of their old vernacular local names.

About two miles north-west of Oldcastle there is a townland called *Fearan na g-cloch* (from peaран, land, and Cloċ, a stone)—so called from two remarkable stone flags still to be seen standing in it, popularly called clocha labaрċha, i. e. "the speaking stones": and these stones also give a local name to the green pasture-field in which they are situated, which is called paірc naȝ-clocha-labaрċha, i. e. "field of the speaking stones."

There can be little doubt that in ancient times the pagan rites of incantation and divination had been practised at these stones, as their very name, so curiously handed down to us, imports: for, in the traditions of the neighbourhood, it is even yet current that they have been consulted in cases where either man or beast was supposed to have been " overlooked"; that they were infallibly effective in curing the consequences of the " evil eye"; and that they were deemed to be unerring in naming the individual through whom these evil consequences came. Even up to a period not very remote, when anything happened to be lost or stolen, these stones were invariably consulted; and, in cases where cattle, &c., had strayed away, the directions they gave for finding them were considered as certain to lead to the desired result. There was one peremptory inhibition, however, to be scrupulously observed in consulting these stones, viz., that they were *never* to be asked to give the same information a second time, as they, under no circumstances whatever, would repeat an answer. It is related that some weary pilgrim who had come, about sixty years ago, from a long distance, to consult these venerable stones, being possessed of that most mischievous of all gifts to mortals—"a bad memory"—after having duly received the answer to the inquiries he had made, but forgetting

The Speaking Stones.

it before he had retired many yards on his return journey—and totally unmindful of the conditions upon which the desired information was obtained—had the temerity to come back and renew his inquiries. Wroth with indignation at this open violation of the terms upon which they condescended to be consulted, " The Speaking Stones" have never since deigned to utter a response.*

It is asserted in the neighbourhood that " The Speaking Stones" originally consisted of four slabs, standing in a right line, three of which existed within the memory of the present inhabitants; but two only

---

* In ancient times so great was the credit given to oracles for foretelling future events, and so sacred were their determinations held, that scarcely any new form of government was instituted, any war waged, any peace concluded, or indeed any business of importance undertaken, without the approbation of some oracle. The answers, of course, were generally expressed in such ambiguous language as might be easily wrested to prove the truth of the oracle, whatever was the event. The most ancient oracle we read of in pagan antiquity was that of Dodona, a town in Epirus; but the most famous was that of Apollo, at Delphi, on the south-west extremity of Mount Parnassus, which we are told by classical authorities often controlled the councils of States, directed the course of armies, and even decided the fate of kingdoms.

now remain, to give testimony to the use in which they were anciently employed. They consist of two thin flags, the northern one, on the right-hand side of the woodcut, being a slab of laminated sandy grit, of an average thickness of eight inches, and rising above ground to the height of about seven feet. Its greatest breadth is five feet eight inches, and at about eighteen inches from the top it begins to taper to a breadth of three feet and a half at the top, which is rudely curved or rounded, as shown in the engraving. At a distance of twenty-five feet southwards, the second stone, which is a blue limestone flag, now leans towards the south-east at an angle of about 45°; but it was, no doubt, originally erected in an upright position. Its height over ground is six feet four inches, and its breadth at base three feet four inches, increasing to four feet eight inches at about four feet from the ground. The thickness at the base is fourteen inches, and the flag tapers to a rudely rounded top, which is only nine inches thick. These two flags, having their flat sides facing east and west, and their thin edges in a direction nearly north and south, stand on the top of a rising embankment or swelling of the ground; and a rath or fort, called *Lis Clogher* (Fort of the stones), is seen in a westerly direction about 300 yards in rear of them. The circumference of this rath measures 588 feet round its base; and it has a rampart or embankment of raised earth about four feet high round its top, inclosing a circular flat space 154 feet in diameter. The fosse or trench surrounding this rath varies in depth from fifteen to twenty-two feet, and is embellished by several venerable old whitethorn trees growing round its margin. In the centre of the rath are caves,* which were opened a few years ago, but are now closed up; and there is every likelihood that within this rath the master-spirit or manipulator of the oracles delivered by "The Speaking Stones" resided in ancient times.

The destruction of the third stone is locally accounted for in the following manner. About the year 1804, Captain Battersby became tenant of the townland of Farannaglogh; and he had a herd or steward, named Blaney, who, supposing that these stones were unnecessarily encumbering the ground, determined to get rid of them. For this purpose, having brought some labourers to the spot, he directed them to break up the stones; but they, from a dread of evil consequences, refused to

---

* Several of the raths of Ireland have been found to contain caves, with narrow passages leading to them, in which it is supposed that stores and corn were kept. Tacitus describes the Germans as having similar repositories for their provisions; while Cæsar says that the Gauls placed their consecrated spoils in such caves. The custom of preserving corn and rice in such subterranean chambers is still practised in Persia and in India. On the hill of Rathbran, in Meath, there is a small artificial cavern traditionally called "the granary," which corresponds exactly with the description of the cave made for keeping paddy or rice, given by Dr. Buchanan in his "Journey in Mysore, &c."; and on this hill is also still to be seen the great stone under whose shelter Fingall and his faithful wolf-dog, Bran, rested, when, in pursuit of a giant, Fingall is said to have walked one morning from Kildare to Sliabh Gullion.

enter upon the work, and this refusal so irritated Blaney that he himself took up a sledge and shivered to pieces the slab which stood about twenty-five feet north of the one represented on the right of the woodcut, the debris of which were buried where they fell. While in the very act of perpetrating this deed of wanton vandalism, word was brought to him that one of his children was drowned in the low grounds to the south of " The Speaking Stones." He ran home in terror, and found his child lifeless, which made such an impression upon him that he never afterwards interfered with the remaining two stones, now still standing, as " solemn silent witnesses" of the mental and social condition of the people in times long past: and it is to be hoped that their history, now made publicly known, will be the means of saving them from future destruction.

The Moat of Oldcastle.

About a quarter of a mile south of Oldcastle, and on the right-hand side of the road leading to Loughcrew, stands The Moat of Oldcastle, named on the Ordnance Map *Mount Fortune ;* but from what cause this modern appellation has been given to it, we have been unable to ascertain. A wall has been raised round it, and it is thus so far protected from injury or destruction; but it has been planted over with fir trees which, though beautiful and picturesque in their proper places, here take away, in an archaeological point of view, from the effect naturally produced by a consideration of its original use; hence the modernly planted trees are wanting in the accompanying sketch and plan of the Moat of Oldcastle.

The height of this artificial mound of earth, constructed in the form of a truncated cone, is twenty feet, and its circumference round the base measures 222 feet, the diameter on the flat top, which, no doubt, was originally circular, varying from thirty-nine to forty-three feet. On its north-west side there is a crescent-shaped plateau of raised earth, about five feet higher than the surrounding ground. The trench which surrounds the Moat, and separates it from the plateau, is from nine to fourteen feet wide, five feet deep at the side adjoining the plateau or glacis, and seventeen feet deep from the top of the Moat. The concave or inner boundary of the crescent-shaped plateau is 120 feet in extent, while its convex or outer boundary measures 324 feet; and the greatest distance between the curved boundaries of the glacis is sixty feet, measured in a north-westerly direction from the Moat. That this Moat, as well as all others of its kind, was constructed in ancient times for the promulgation of various laws, ordinances, and enactments, there can be no manner of doubt, the lawgiver standing on the top of the Moat, and those who were to receive and carry out the law standing on the glacis in front of him, and facing the sun one of the divinities probably worshipped at the time of its erection.

The name is said to be derived from the Celtic word Moóp (pronounced *Maught*), meaning *Court of justice, meeting*, or *assembly*. We find the word still used in the Scottish Highlands; and the most idiomatic Gaelic for "The Day of Judgment", is La mhoíò (pronounced *voyt*). In Scotland these mounds are often called Mote-hills; and, as we are informed in Macpherson's "Antiquities of Scotland," p. 169, in the Scottish Highlands they are called Mute-hills, i. e., Word-hills, or places for deliberation. Such hills of assembly in Meath will at once be recognised not only in the one under present consideration, but also in the Moats of Dervor, Donaghpatrick, Navan, and some others.

In our own days, so far as we know, the last place in which the ancient practice is still observed is in the Isle of Man, on *Tynwald Hill*, a name derived from the Icelandic *tinga*, " to speak," and *valld*, "a hill," on which, though not the seat of Government, and, in fact, little more than a locality, the Governor is situated when he ratifies, and then promulgates, certain laws which have been already agreed upon by the legislature of the Island.

The following account of the mode of promulgating the laws in the Isle of Man is quoted from "A Descriptive and Historical Account of the Isle of Man; with a view of its Society, Manners, and Customs, partly compiled from various Authorities and from Observations made in a Tour through the Island in the summer of 1808. Dedicated to His Majesty: to which is prefixed a Map of the Isle of Man. Printed for the Author (*whose name is not given*), by Preston and Heaton, Newcastle-upon-Tyne, 1809," p. 113, &c. :—

"Tynwald Hill, a barrow of a conical-shape and regular construction, has been rendered illustrious by the use to which it has long been applied. A flight of grassy steps fronting the Chapel of St. John leads up to the summit; below are three circular turf seats, for the different orders of the people; the lowest is about four feet wide, and eighty yards in circumference. The superior seats diminish of course, according to their height (from the conical form of the Mount), while on the extreme top, which is about two yards in diameter, is occasionally placed a chair under a canopy of state.

" This singular Mount stands upon a lawn called St. John's Green, nearly in the centre of the Isle of Man, and has a very picturesque appearance from any of the four cross roads which meet here. It is situated in a beautiful and richly cultivated valley, surrounded by high mountains, and the whole forms a most delightful landscape, of which the sea does not form any part.

" At the top of this Mount, Sir John Stanley (an ancestor of the Earl of Derby), King and Lord of Man, convened the whole body of the people to hear the promulgation of the laws, which, till then, were locked up in the breasts of the Deemsters (Judges).

" In some degree the Tynwald Mount is still the scene of legislation ; for, whatever respects the internal polity of the Island must, by immemorial usage, be published at this place.

" The following is an account of the forms observed at the Tynwald Hill a few years since, with the order of procession which attended the Duke of Athol. Agreeable to ancient custom, every parish sent four horsemen, properly accoutred, and the Captain of every parish presided over those of his own district. About eleven o'clock the cavalcade arrived at St. John's, when the Duke of Athol was received by the Clergy and Keys, and saluted by the fencibles. He then went in state to the chapel on St. John's Green, where a sermon was preached. After service followed the procession of State. The fencibles were drawn up in two lines, from the chapel door to the Tynwald Hill, and the procession passed between the lines in the following order :—

The Clergy, two and two, the juniors first,
The Lord Bishop of Sodor and Man,
The Vicars General,
The two Deemsters,
The Sword-bearer with the Sword of State,
His Grace the Duke of Athol,
The Lieutenant Governor,
The Clerk of the Rolls,
The twenty-four Keys, two and two,
The Captains of the different Parishes.

" As soon as His Grace had ascended the Hill, he was seated under the canopy in his Chair of State, and the Deemsters then proceeded to the ordinary business of the day. The new laws were read in English, and then in Manks ; and after all the business of the Hill was gone through, three cheers were given to His Grace, the Lord Lieutenant and Governor-in-Chief. His Grace then descended from the Hill, and the procession moved back again to the chapel in the same regular order. After the necessary business was finished in the chapel, such as signing the Laws, &c., His Grace was conducted to his coach and six, and returned to his residence.

" In former times a Court was regularly held here on St. John's Day, when every person had a right to present any particular grievance, and to have his complaint heard in the face of the whole country."

Keeping in mind the difference of time and circumstances, from the foregoing we can form some idea of the mode, attended of course with much less pomp and paraphernalia, in which the laws of ancient Erin were promulgated from many a Moat still existing in the country.

The parish of Loughcrew has derived its name from a lake called Loch Cꞃaoιbe,' i. e. the lake of the tree; but the name of *creeve* was only applied in the old vernacular language of the country to such

places as " *had originally a sacred tree of widely extending branches,*"* and
around which " religious rites were celebrated."†

Loch Cpaoibe.‡

This lake is situated about 200 perches from Loughcrew House, a
beautiful building in the Ionic style, and has a small companion lake
adjoining, both nearly in the south-western corner of a demesne of
more than 1000 acres in extent, of which at least 200 acres are under
plantation. A more solemn spot than the shores of this lake, em-
bosomed in hills often seen mirrored on its tranquil surface, present for
the celebration of religious ceremonies, could scarcely be imagined :
and it is to be regretted that the exact site, in or around the lake,
where this ancient venerable tree once stood cannot now be ascertained.
Probably it flourished on the small island in the larger lake, a view of
which is here presented.

---

* Dr. O'Donovan's Letter on Loughcrew during the Progress of the Ordnance
Survey : see Appendix, p. 47.
† Dr. Joyce's " Origin and History of Irish Names of Places," p. 483.
‡ Pronounced *Lough Creevy.* The beautiful lake scene here represented has been
engraved by Mr. Cooper, London, from a photograph taken by Mr. Chancellor, Dublin,
on 10th August, 1870 ; and the two preceding views of "The Speaking Stones," and
" The Moat of Oldcastle," have been engraved by Mr. Oldham, Dublin, from sketches
most obligingly made for us by Mr. Andrew Smyth, one of the teachers in the Oldcastle
Endowed Schools.

In all probability the trees held most sacred in Ireland were the hazel, and the mountain ash, or rowan tree; and in England the oak and the elm. We are told in Dr. Joyce's " Origin and History of Irish Names of Places," p. 495, that " Mac Cuill (literally ' son of the hazel,') one of the three last Kings of the Tuatha de Dananns, was so called because he worshipped the hazel;" and in an earlier portion of this highly interesting and instructive volume, at p. 482, he shows that the ancient Irish also had trees under which their chiefs used to be inaugurated : —

"Trees of this kind were regarded with intense reverence and affection ; one of the greatest triumphs that a tribe could achieve over their enemies was to cut down this inauguration tree, and no outrage was more keenly resented, or when possible, visited with sharper retribution. Our Annals often record their destruction as events of importance; at 981 for example, we read in the Four Masters, that the *bile* of *Magh-adhar* (Mah-oyre) in Clare—the great tree under which the O'Briens were inaugurated—was rooted out of the earth, and cut up, by Malachy, King of Ireland ; and at 1111, that the Ulidians led an army to Tullahogue, the inauguration place of the O'Neills, and cut down the old trees; for which Niall O'Loughlin afterwards exacted a retribution of 3000 cows."

After the introduction of Christianity into England, we find that both the civil and the ecclesiastical authorities passed enactments condemning the worship of trees, and this occurred even at no more remote a period than in the reign of Canute.*

That the worship of trees was not peculiar either to Ireland or to England, but that it was of world-wide extent, we may observe that the Assyrian Sculptures in the British Museum afford us numerous representations of the worship of trees. In Fergusson's " Picturesque Illustrations of Ancient Architecture," reference is made to one of the sculptured panels of the gateway of the Sanchi Monument, on which the worship of a tree is represented. Under the sanction and assistance of the Indian Council, the same gifted author, James Fergusson, Esq., D. C. L., F. R. S., &c., has more recently brought out a large volume,† embellished with numerous engravings and photographs. Space only permits us here to refer to this elaborate work, which contains valuable explanatory essays illustrating the mythological sculptures adorning the ancient remains of Buddhist architecture now existing in Central India, viz., in the Topes or Funeral Mounds of Sanchi and Amravati.

Colonel Forbes Leslie‡ gives a beautiful illustration and a most interesting history and description of the sacred fig-tree at Anuradhapoora, the ancient capital of Ceylon, to which tree Buddhist pilgrims

---

* Colonel Forbes Leslie's " Early Races of Scotland," p. 171.
† " Tree and Serpent Worship, or Illustrations of Mythology and Art in India in the first and fourth centuries after Christ."
‡ " Early Races of Scotland," p. 173, *et seq.*

still resort to pay their devotions, the tree being known, from the self-renovating powers peculiar to the *Ficus religiosa*, to have maintained itself for the past twenty-one centuries.

We now approach the consideration of the grandest of all the remains of pagan antiquity in the neighbourhood—one of the ancient royal cemeteries of Ireland—which we ourselves had the good fortune to bring to light.

On Tuesday, the 9th of June, 1863, we paid our first accidental visit to the Loughcrew Hills, popularly and, indeed, geographically known as Sliabh na Caillighe; and finding the various summits of the range for two miles in extent studded with the remains of ancient carns, or tombs, we were afterwards fortunate enough to interest the proprietor, the late James Lenox William Naper, Esq., and his agent, Charles William Hamilton, Esq., in the discovery we had made: and through them we were enabled to make a systematic examination of this great primeval cemetery, then nameless and unknown; but which, as we shall see presently, once had a name and history of no mean repute.

On the 23rd May and 14th November, 1864, and on 26th February, 1866, we had the honour of making communications to the Royal Irish Academy on the subject—an abstract account of the results of which is printed in Volume IX., p. 355, &c. of the Proceedings R. I. A.

During the month of July, 1867, we employed a first-rate professional artist to draw, under our own eye and correction, all the curious and remarkable devices on the numerous large stones forming the interior chambers in these carns: and it has proved fortunate that we did so at a period when most of these were clear and unmistakable, after being recently exposed; for, at our latest visit to the place, we found instances, from the effects of subsequent weathering, where it would be now impossible to draw the original devices with accuracy and fidelity.

The wild legend that a witch had scattered these great heaps of stones out of her apron has been doing duty in this locality, from time immemorial, for the real name and history of the place; and probably would have continued for many a day longer to perpetuate the fanciful story, had not James Fergusson, Esq., &c., on 16th of August, 1870, carefully gone over the hills under our guidance.

This practised explorer, acute observer, and clear-minded author has since published* a large volume, entitled "Rude Stone Monuments in all Countries: their Age and Uses"—in our opinion the best written, and best arranged book ever published upon the subject of which it treats. In this profusely illustrated Work he has the honour of being the first to suggest, and he deserves the hearty thanks of every Irish Archæologist for having done so, that these carns must be the remains of the cemetery of Taillten, this happy thought thus affording

---

* John Murray, Albemarle-street, London, 1872.

B

the means, we hope, of restoring a name and history to the great and forgotten "city of the dead" on the heights now called the Loughcrew
Hills.

In a case such as this, we think it would be unfair to paraphrase
the author's account of his original attempt to identify the place; and,
therefore, we quote Mr. Fergusson's opinions in his own words.

After giving some account of the examination of these carns by us
during the summer of 1865, and the various objects found there, he
then proceeds:—

"It now only remains to try to ascertain who those were who
were buried in these tumuli, and when they were laid there to their rest.
So far as the evidence at present stands it hardly seems to me to admit
of doubt but that this is the cemetery of Talten, so celebrated in Irish
legend and poetry:—

> ' The host of Great Meath are buried,
>   In the middle of the Lordly Brugh;
>   The Great Ultonians used to bury
>   At Talten with pomp.

> ' The true Ultonians, before Conchobor,
>   Were ever buried at Talten,
>   Until the death of that triumphant man,
>   Through which they lost their glory.'*

" The distance of the spot from Telltown, the modern representa-
tive of Talten, is twelve miles, which to some might appear an objection; but it must be remembered that Brugh is ten miles from Tara,
where all the kings resided, who were buried there; and as Dathi and
others of them were buried at Rath Croghan, sixty-five miles off,
distance seems hardly to be an objection. Indeed, among a people
who, as evidenced by their monuments, paid so much attention to
funeral rites and ceremonious honours to their dead, as the pagan
Irish evidently did, it must have mattered little whether the last resting place of one of their kings was a few miles nearer or farther from
his residence.

" It must not, however, be forgotten, that the proper residence of
the Ultonians, who are said to have been buried at Talten, was
Emania or Armagh, forty-five miles distant as the crow flies. Why
they should choose to be buried in Meath, so near the rival capital of
Tara, if that famous city then existed, is a mystery which it is not
easy to solve; but that it was so, there seems no doubt, if the traditions or books of the Irish are at all to be depended upon. If their
real residence was so distant, it seems of trifling consequence whether
it was ten or twelve miles from the place we now know as Telltown.
There must have been some very strong reason for inducing the
Ultonians to bury so far from their homes; but as that reason has not
been recorded, it is idle to attempt to guess what form it took. What

---

* Petrie's "Round Towers," p. 105.

would appear a most reasonable suggestion to a civilized Saxon in the nineteenth century would, in all probability, be the direct antithesis of the motive that would guide an uncivilized Celt in the first century before Christ, and we may therefore as well give up the attempt. Some other reason than that of mere proximity to the place of residence governed the Irish in the choice of the situation of their cemeteries; what that was we may hereafter be able to find out; at present, so far as I know, the materials do not exist for forming an opinion. If, however, this is not Talten, no graves have been found nearer Telltown which would at all answer to the description that remains to us of this celebrated cemetery; and, till they are found, these Loughcrew mounds seem certainly entitled to the distinction. I cannot see that the matter is doubtful."*

A little further on we hope to be able to help Mr. Fergusson to a solution of some of the doubts and difficulties which he feels in establishing his hypothesis; and, in the meantime, we must say that we entirely agree with him in thinking that he has truly identified the ancient royal cemetery of Taillten with the series of carns on the Loughcrew Hills. So far as we can see there is no other way of accounting for the extensive remains of so large a necropolis at that place; and, if a better hypothesis can be established, no one will more sincerely rejoice at it than Mr. Fergusson and ourselves. If, however, this is not the site of the cemetery of Taillten, of the existence of which we have such positive documentary evidence, *where is it? or by what other name can this great cemetery be called?* for there are no indications of pagan burial at, or nearer to, the place we now call Telltown.

That this latter place may have been the scene of the celebration of various games, aquatic sports, races, and, according to tradition, the far-famed "Telltown marriage" ceremony,† we see no reason to dispute.

---

* Fergusson's " Rude Stone Monuments," p. 219.

† The parish of Telltown is situate in the Barony of Upper Kells; and, according to the Ordnance Survey, has an area of 4266A. 0R. 34P. statute measure, containing a townland, also called Telltown, of 626 acres in extent. In this townland, about sixty perches north of the River Blackwater, and about twice that distance north of Telltown House, is a very remarkable Rath, called Rᴀᴄʜ Ꝺubli (*Black Rath*), measuring 334 yards round its base, which will make it occupy an area of 1A. 3R. 13P.; while its circumference on top, measuring 307 yards, gives an area of 1A. 2R. 8P. statute measure. The slant height of this artificially raised tableland on the north is 17 ft. 4 in., north-west 17 ft., west 17 ft. 6 in., south-west 15 ft., south 21 ft. 3 in., south-east 18 ft., and on the east 12 ft. The north-east side of the rath has been levelled, for the purpose, evidently, of facilitating access to it: and on the south side an excavation has been made, 15 yards in breadth, extending 12 yards inwards; but at what period we are unable to state. There are MS. accounts of several royal residences being erected for Taillte by her husband, the Monarch Eochaidh Garbh, who is recorded to have made her presents of *Palaces*, *Grianans*, *Duns*, and lands : and we think it highly probable that this great rath was the site of one of the principal royal residences of Queen Taillte, and that to this fact both the townland and parish may owe their names.

Among the other remains of antiquity still to be seen at Telltown are traces of three artificial lakes ; and, about forty perches north-west of the spot pointed out as

We are, however, not disposed to concur in the hitherto popularly received opinion that the great Fair of Taillten was held at the modern Telltown, which lies in a remarkably low situation, on the banks of the Blackwater, nearly midway between Kells and Navan.

It is well known that an annual meeting of the people, called in Irish Oenach* (*Fair*)†, was usually held at their Regal cemeteries: and we submit that the epithet applied to the cemetery of Taillten, in the following quotation, could not only not apply to the place now known as Telltown, singularly destitute of hills as it is, but will accurately describe the site of the cemetery at present under consideration.

Flannagan,‡ King of Bregia in Meath, a man of no small distinction in his time, and to whom the locality must have been well known, referring to the death of Cleò ꝑhιnnliaċ (*Aedh Fhinnliath*)§, Sovereign of Ireland, on 20th November, 876, after recounting his various peculiarities and admirable qualities, styles him in the following two lines of poetry :—

Ɣꝛaιꝑnιò Caιlcen celɣlaιne,   "Master of the games of the *fair-hilled* Taillten,
Rí Ceaṁꝛaċ cꝛeꝑ co cecaιò.   King of Teamhair (Tara) of an hundred conflicts."‖

From this we can infer three facts : first, that the site of the cemetery of Taillten, though forgotten in the 19th, was well known in the 9th century ; second, that games, presided over by the Sovereign of Ireland, were celebrated at it; and last, but most important point of all for its present identification, that the cemetery was situated on some *fair hills*.

The fair of Taillten, with its attendant games and sports, we are informed by The Four Masters, was established in honor of his foster-mother, *Taillte*, by the celebrated King, Lugh Lamhfhada¶ (Lewy of

---

" the vale of marriage," two earthen mounds, popularly known as " the knockans," but which tradition says constitutes " the hill of separation." The distance between the bases of the two mounds, which run parallel, is about ten feet ; and the gradual slope at each end affords an easy mode of ascent and descent. The length of the southern mound is 235 feet ; its greatest slant height on the northern side is 22¼ feet, and on the southern side 33¼ feet. The length of the northern mound is 340 feet, greatest slant height on northern side 34 feet, and on southern side 10 feet. It has been said that in pagan times those who had contracted a " Telltown marriage" might, " after a year and a day," cancel their contract, if so disposed, by simply marching up these mounds and turning their backs upon one another,

* Pronounced *Aynagh.*
† Petrie's " Round Towers," p. 107.
‡ " Four Masters," A. D. 876, 890, 891.
§ Pronounced *Ae Finlay.*
‖ " Four Masters," A. D. 876, vol. i. p. 524.
¶ The Four Masters state :—" It was in the reign of this Lugh that the fair of Taillten was established, in commemoration and remembrance of his foster mother, *Taillte*, the daughter of Maghmor, King of Spain, and the wife of Eochaidh, son of Erc, the last King of the Firbolgs."
(*See* Dr. O'Donovan's " Annals of Ireland," by The Four Masters, vol. i., p. 22,)

the Long Hand), who, according to the same authority, died* B. C. 1829, i. e. thirty-seven centuries ago.

Although this fair, the greatest of all the annual gatherings of the Irish people, was usually held with great pomp, commencing on the first day of August, it was occasionally, from civil discords, or other causes, interrupted or prevented,† and at other times renewed,‡ by different sovereigns.

From the account of its last celebration, under Roderic O'Conor, last Monarch of Ireland, who died at Cong, A. D. 1198, we make the following extract:—

Aonac Caillcen ımoρρo bo bénaṁ la ρíᵹ Eρeann ocuρ la Leć Chuınn bon cuρ ρın ocuρ ρo Leċρecc a n-ᵹρaıρne ocuρ a maρcρluaᵹ ó Mullać Aıbı ᵹo Mullać Caıcen.

"On this occasion the Fair of Taillten was celebrated by the King of Ireland and the people of Leath-Chuinn,§ and their horses and cavalry were spread out on the space extending from Mullach-Aidi to Mullach-Taiten (? Taillten)."
Four Masters, Vol. ii. A. D. 1168.

The Hill of Lloyd, 422 feet above the sea level, situated west of Kells, and in a direct line towards Sliabh na Caillighe, is still known by the Irish-speaking population as "Mullach Aidi," or Aide's Hill. ‖ As to Mullach Taillten, or the summit of the cemetery of Taillten, Dr. O'Donovan, the editor and translator of the Annals of Ireland by the Four Masters, points out, in a note upon this passage, that there is an error in the text in writing *Taiten* for *Taillten;* and, as there is no Mullach, or hill, at Telltown, nor any remains of a cemetery, round which such annual gatherings as we are referring to were customarily held, it is not by any means probable that "their horses and cavalry were spread out on the space extending from" the Hill of Lloyd to Telltown, a line of country, moreover, unsuited and rather impracticable for such a purpose. On the contrary, standing on the summit of Mullach Aidi, or Hill of Lloyd, and looking in a direct line to the summit of Sliabh na Caillighe, which we think we may fairly take the liberty of calling Mullach Taillten, at a distance of 6 or 7 miles, there

---

* It ought to be observed that some persons doubt the great antiquity ascribed to some of our early Irish celebrities ; but, we take the statements of the Annalists for what they are worth, and will be glad, in the interests of truth, to see them overturned, if such can be done, by better documentary evidence, whenever that can be produced.

† Four Masters, A. D. 806, 825, 925.

‡ Four Masters, A. D. 894, 915, 1006.

§ Pronounced *Lea Queene* (the northern half of Ireland).

‖ About half a mile west of Kells, and on the highest point of the hill, stands a handsome round stone pillar, commonly known as "The Pillar of Lloyd." It was erected in 1791, by the first Earl of Bective, in memory of his father, the Right Hon. Sir Thomas Taylor, Bart. It is upwards of 100 feet in height, with a projecting balcony on top, fenced in by an iron railing, and surmounted by a glass dome. Inside a spiral stone staircase, containing 202 steps, each about six inches in height, protected by an iron hand railing, leads to the top, from which there is a charming view of the surrounding country.

is stretched out before the observer one of the most beautiful plains the eye could rest upon, and one exactly suited to the gathering of such a hosting.

In confirmation of this opinion, it should be observed that we have still existing proof that the cemetery was not exclusively confined to the Loughcrew Hills; for, as we proceed thence in the direction of Lloyd, on an eminence about two miles distant, called "King's Mountain," we find in the middle of a large pasture-field, now set up as a rubbing stone for cattle, a flagstone, with spirals or volutes inscribed upon it, measuring 7½ feet in height, 3 feet wide, and about 6 inches in uniform thickness. On its present site, up to a few years ago, stood a tumulus, which the proprietor of the field caused to be carried away for top-dressing; and in the centre of the mound this stone was found, covering in a chamber formed of smaller flagstones, and filled with bones, all of which have disappeared, the covering stone alone excepted.

Approaching still nearer to Lloyd, and about four miles distant from it, we have in the townland of Clonsilla the remains of two carns and some large upright stones, all within a few perches of one another; so that, while the "horses and cavalry," above referred to, occupied this valley, they were actually standing around some of the tombs.

It is a very remarkable coincidence that up to a recent period, and, indeed, not yet quite given up, a large annual gathering of the people, or "Patron," extending westwards from St. Kieran's Church and Well, was held in this plain during the first week of August (the period of the year for the celebration of the famous Fair of Taillten): and this is the more remarkable inasmuch as the festival of St. Kieran, which would be the day naturally and usually set apart for the celebration of the "Patron," in honour of the patron Saint of the parish, occurs on the 14th June, the recorded date of Saint Kieran's death.

On the same plain, still further westward, and in the direction of Sliabh na Caillighe, the Fair of Balgree was formerly held. It extended from within half a mile east of the Virginia Road Station, on the Oldcastle branch of the Dublin and Drogheda Railway, to Cloughan-rush—a space of about two statute miles in length. No Fair, however, has been held here within the memory of the oldest inhabitant, although it continues to be published in the advertised lists of Fairs.

Approaching nearer to Sliabh na Caillighe, on the same plain, we find that the ancient Oenach has transmitted its memories to us in the modernly spelled name of the townland of *Enagh,* on the Cavan estate of the Marquis of Headfort, there being also two other townlands of the same name not far distant.

It has not, we believe, been satisfactorily ascertained where queen *Taillte,* was buried; and, in the absence of any proof to the contrary, we think it is very likely that her tomb was placed upon one of the summits known as Sliabh na Caillighe; and that from this fact the cemetery may have been called *The Cemetery of Taillte.*

Now, if this were the case, we might be able to connect in some way, though not in the literal sense of the terms of the modern local legend, the name—Sliabh na Caillighe—or "the old woman's mountain," with the fact of the mountain being the site of Taillte's tomb. All this, of course, is purely conjectural, but, we think, highly probable.

Brian O'Looney, Esq., M.R.I.A., of the Catholic University, Dublin, has most obligingly favoured us with the following interesting extract from the Book of Lecan, accompanied by a translation :—

THE FAIR OF TAILLTEN.

(*Dindsencas, from Book of Lecan, fol.* 258, *a. a.*)

" Cailltin canur po h-ainmnigeb . nin, Cailltiu ingen Mag Moin bean eachaċ Ṡaiṁb meic Duaċ Temin ar leir bo ṗonab Duma na n-Ṡiall a Cempaiṁ ocur ba h-ı rin buıṁe Loṁa Maıc an Scaıl baılb ocur ırı conacaıb ror a ceıli Caıll Chuaın bo rlaıṁı comab aenach imo leċc ccur abbach rı a kalamb auṁaırb ıar rin ocur po caċc a ṁuba ocur a nárab la Luṁaıb . unbe Luṁ-narab bicınr. [bicıcur] u. c. blıabaın ımorro, crı mılı rı n-ṁeın Crırc anbrın ocur no ṁnıcha an c-aenaċ rın la cach rıṁ no ṁeıbeab Eren co caınıṁ Pabraıṁ; ocur . cccc. blıabaın a Cailltın o Pabraıṁ co bub aenaċ Donbchaba mac Flaınb meıc Maelrechlaınb. Ceora ṁera bo Cailltein: [.ı.] ceċc crıchı.can caırrlım, a beċraın car clé ṁualaınb, ocur urchar nab ṁneama ıncı uınbı Aenach Cailltean bicıcur, bıa n-ebrab ro :—

" Taillten, why so called? Answer: Tailtiu, daughter of Magh Mor, the wife of Eochaidh Garbh, son of Duach Temin; it was by him Duma na n-Giall, at Temair, was made, and she was the nurse (foster-mother) of Lugaidh, son of Scal Balbh, and it was she that *requested her husband to cut down Caill Cuain, that it should be an Oenach (a fair or assembly-place) around her Leacht (or grave),* and she died on the Kalend of August after that, and her *guba* (lamentations) and her *nosad* (games—funeral rites) were celebrated by *Lugad, unde Lug Nosad dicitur.* Five hundred years, moreover, and three thousand before the birth of Christ this occurred, and this fair was made (celebrated) by every king who occupied Erin till Patrick came. And four hundred years [it continued to be celebrated] in Taillten, from Patrick to the Black Fair of Donchadh, son of Fland, son of Maelseachlaind. Three prohibitions were upon Taillten [namely], to pass through it without alighting; to see it over the left shoulder; and to throw a cast which does not take effect in it—*unde* the Fair of Taillten dicitur — of which is said as follows :—

I.

A chaema ċrıchı ċuın Caın, Eırcıṁ rınb ar benbaċcaın ; Co n-ınbırer baıb rençar ren Suıṁ[b]ıuṁub aenaıṁ Cailltern.

I.

You nobles of the land of comely Conn, Listen to us for our blessing ; Till I relate to you the ancient history Of the origin of the fair of Tailtiu.

II.

Cailcıu ınṁen Mab Moın Moıll, bean eachaċ ṁaırb mac Duaċ Daıll, Cucab runb re rluaṁ Fer m-bolṁ, Co Caıll Cuan ıar ċaċ comarb.

II.

Tailtiu, daughter of renowned Magh Mor, Wife of Eochaidh Garbh, son of Duach Dall, Was thither brought by the Firbolg host, To *Caill Cuain,* after a co-valiant battle.

III.

Caill Ċuan bo ba ċleċcup cpanb
O Eipcip co h-Aċ n-Opumann
O Monaiʒ Moip meb n-uibi
O Aill co h-Apb na Suiʒi.

III.

Caill Cuain, tall and stately were its trees
[Extended] from *Eisgir* to *Ath n-Droman ;*
From *Monad More*, of great adventures;
From *Aill* to *Ard na-Suigi* (hill of the Suck).

IV.

A Suiʒi an Suiʒi Sealʒa
Cop n-bailbip Daim Opuim Oepʒa
Ʒnaċ ceann capbaib a caill paip
I n-Aċ Finb a Cuil Clochaip.

IV.

From *Suige (Suck)* of the *Suighe Scalga*,
Whither went the *Dams** of *Druim Dearg ;*
From the wood eastward the chariot head did pass
Into *Ath Find* to [from] *Cuil Clochar.*

V.

Comap Cuppach cenb line
Apb m-banba a m-bibip pinbi
babap copcpaib coin Caipppi
Op op Cippa Munʒaipʒi.

V.

The confluence† of Curach, the head of the river,
The hill of *Banba*, where spears were wont to be,
The hounds of Cairpri were triumphant
Over the borders of *Tipra Mungarge.‡*

VI.

Mop bo ʒnepaib bo ʒeinncib,
Do ċpepaib bo ċpom Ceinnceib
A cup Cailleab Cuan cap cenn
Pa paeċpach pluaiʒ pep n-Epen.

VI.

Many the heroes of the pagans,
The battles (battalions), the great fires,
That were engaged in felling *Caill Cuain*,
Delightful was the host of the Firbolgs.

felix ḣ Ġuinn

VII.

O chobaċc lé an ċaill ċain
Cona ppemaib a calmain
Ria cinb bliabna ba bpeʒ Muiʒ
ba maʒ pcochab pcoċpempaiʒ.

* * * * * *

VII.

When she had felled the beautiful wood,
And having cleared its roots out of the ground,
Before the end of one year it was *Breg Muigh*,
It was a flowery plain adorned with shamrocks."§

* * * * * *

XXII.

Maipib mup caillcen caċ ċan
In po abnaċc can impal
Ocup mup pulainʒ mop mapb
Inb po abnaċc eoċaib ʒapb.

XXII.

The *mur* of Tailtin survives all time
In which she was buried without doubt
And a *mur* which conceals multitudes of dead—
In which was buried Eochaidh Garbh.

XXIII.

Pop mup eachaċ pnaiʒċi clach
Fiċċe popab piʒ cempaċ.
Ocup pop mup punn amna
Fiċċe popab a piʒna.

XXIII.

Upon the *mur* of Eochaidh of chiselled stone
Are the twenty mounds of the kings of Temar,
And on the *mur* of his wife, there also
Are the twenty mounds of their queens.

XXIV.

Riʒ-impcinʒ bo'n mumain muaib
Pop piʒu cempaċ a cuaib.
Ceopa Connaċc cib nab caċ
Pop popab pep olneʒmaċc.

XXIV.

A kingly *Imscing* for noble Munster
By the kings of Temar on the north.   [talion
The three [mounds] of Connaught—almost a bat-
Upon the *Forud* of the men of *Olnegmacht.* ‖

---

* Companies.   † The meeting of the two rivers.
‡ Fountain or stream of *Mungarg.*
§ Whoever can, from the foregoing, or other sources, identify at the present time
the position, extent, and limits of this great wood, called Caill Cuain, in the centre
of which Taillte is here stated to have been buried, will contribute much to the
history and topography of the renowned Taillten. The site of the wood, which
probably covered the hills as well as the plains, was afterwards called *Magh Taillten*
(Taillte's plain), and *Breg Magh* (beautiful plain): but, from all this, we see no
reason to alter our opinion that Taillte's Tomb may have been situated on the range
of hills which is on all sides surrounded by the most beautiful plains, and which
may very naturally have constituted the centre of the great wood of Cuan. Indeed
we feel rather fortified in our opinion by the most valuable and ingenious remarks

We have documentary authority for stating that the Irish, in pagan times, had regal cemeteries in various parts of the island, appropriated to the interment of the chiefs or princes of the different races who ruled, either as sole monarchs or as provincial kings. This valuable authority is preserved in a tract called Senchap na Relec,* or History of the Cemeteries, being a fragment of the oldest and most celebrated Irish Manuscript we possess—viz., Leabhap na h-Uiohpi,† which is a collection of pieces in prose and verse, compiled and transcribed at Clonmacnois, about A. D. 1100, by *Moelmuiri Mac Ceileachair,*‡ grandson of Conn na m-bocht, a distinguished writer of that great abode of learning. In quoting this tract Dr. Petrie§ remarks that— "judging from its language, its age must be referred to a period several centuries earlier than that in which its transcriber flourished. It is also to be observed that this tract is glossed in its original, evidently by *Moelmuiri* himself, and that such explanations of the transcriber are given within crotchets, both in the Irish text and the translation of it."

From this venerable old authority we cull the following extracts, in which mention occurs of the cemetery of Taillten :—

Ropcap iác po cpí ppiám peilce h-Epenb pía cpecim, .i. Cpuacu, " These were the three chief cemeteries of Erin before the Faith (i. e. before the introduction of Christianity), viz. —

---

of Mr. O'Looney upon the foregoing poem ; as from a new point of view, they may supply an interesting key to the inquiry as to the position of Taillten, and an additional argument in favour of the theory advanced in these pages :—" Were we to indulge a little in etymological conjecture, based on the phonetic analogy between the genitive forms, *Caille* (of the wood), and *Caillighe* (of the old woman), we might be pardoned for suggesting that *Sliabh na Caille* (the mountain of the wood)was the true and original name of the mountain ; and that the wood from which it got the name, and of which it may have been a part, was, perhaps, the *Caill Cuain* (wood of Cuan) mentioned in the poem on the Fair of Taillten. The change of *Caille* (of the wood) to *Caillighe* (of the old woman) would be a very natural consequence of the decay and disuse of the Irish language in this district at a very early period, and of the adoption of an irregular or false accentuation—e.g., if the final *e* of *Caille,*which is short, be pronounced long, the whole change is phonetically accomplished, as long *e* or *é* has the same sound as *ighe,* and there is reason to suppose that the present anglicised form *Sliabh na Caillighe* is based on and preserves the phonetic form of the word. Without even urging that *Caillighe* is a corruption of Caille, it would be quite in harmony with ancient usage, that when the wood was cut down by desire of *Taillte,* the queen, and *Caillech,* or nurturer of so many distinguished persons in her time, she selected this delightful eminence of *Sliabh na Caille* (mountain of the wood) for her last abode, and hence the place was called *Sliabh na Caillighe,* or mountain of the old woman, *Taillte;* from which came the name *Taillten,* an appellation still surviving, while the original name *Sliabh na Caille* (or mountain of the wood) became extinct with the wood itself."—B. O'L.

‖ For a full enumeration and description of the mounds, graves, and monuments of *Tailtin, Brugh na Boinne,* and other ancient cemeteries, see O'Curry's Lectures on the Manners and Customs of the People of Ancient Erin, edited with Introduction, Notes and Appendices, by W. K. Sullivan, Ph. D., Secretary of the Royal Irish Academy, and Professor of Chemistry to the Catholic University of Ireland, and to the Royal College of Science. 3 vols. complete.

   * Pronounced *Shanahus na relick.*   † Pronounced *Lebur na heera.*
   ‡ Pronounced *Maolmurra Mac Kealaher.*   § " Round Towers," p. 97.

ın bnuz, ın Caıllcıu, Luaċaıp Aılbe, Oénaċ Aılbe, Oénaċ Culı, Oénaċ Colman, Cemaıp Epanb."—*Leabhar na h-Uidhri*, p. 51, col. 1.

Cruachu, Brugh, Taillten, Luachair Ailbe, Oenach Ailbe, Oenach Culi, Oenach Colmain, Temhair Erann."— *Leabhar na h-Uidhri*, p. 51, col. 1.

* * * *

* * * * *

h-ı Callcın, ımoppo, no h-abnaıccıp Ulaıb .ı. Ollam Póċla co na ċlaınb, co canıc Conċoboṕ, .ı. aṕ ıṕ anb ṕo ċoʒṕıbe a ċabaıṕc eceṕ ṕlea ⁊ muıṕ, ⁊ aıʒeb ṕaıṕ, Póbéıʒ na cṕeıcmı ṕom bóı.—*Leabhar na h-Uidhri*, p. 51, col. 2, top.

" At Taillten the Kings of Ulster were used to bury, viz., Ollamh Fodhla, with his descendants, down to Conchobhor, who wished that he should be carried to a place between Slea and the Sea, with his face to the east, on account of the Faith which he had embraced."— *Leabhar na h-Uidhri*, p. 51, col. 2, top.

In *Leabhar na h-Uidhri* there is also a tract on the death and burial at Rathcroghan of Dathi, the last pagan monarch of Ireland, in which occurs a poem, ascribed to Dorban, a poet of West Connaught, from which the following three stanzas are extracted :—

Iac cṕı ṕéılce Iolaıbe
Relec Cħaılcen, ṕe coʒa,
Relec Cṕúaċan ṕíṕ ʒlaıne
Ocuṕ ṕelec ın bṕoʒa.

" The three cemeteries of Idolaters are
The cemetery of Taillten, the select,
The ever-clean cemetery of Cruachan
And the cemetery of Brugh.

Abnaıċce ṕlóʒ ṕo Mıbı
Aṕ láṕ ın bṕoʒa cúaċaıʒ;
No abnaſccıṕ aṕb Ulaıb
Iṕ ın Calcın co lúaċaıṕ.

The host of great Meath were buried
In the middle of the lordly Brugh;
The great Ultonians used to bury
At Taillten with pomp.

Pıṕ Ulaıb, ṕıa Conċoboṕ,
Abnaıċce h-ı Calcın ṕıam,
Co baṕ ınb ṕıṕ ṕoṕbaṕaıʒ,
Dıa n-beaċaıb bıb a nıam.
Leabhar na h-Uidhri, p. 38, col. 2.

The true Ultonians, before Conchobhor,
Were ever buried at Taillten,
Until the death of that triumphant man,
Through which they lost their glory."
Leabhar na h-Uidhri, p. 38, col. 2.

This poem in *Leabhar na h-Uidhri* is followed by a prose Commentary, both given by Moelmuiri on the authority of the ancient accounts collected by Eochaihd Eolach O'Ceirin and Flann, from which we extract the following passage, showing who were buried at Taillten :—

Maċı Ulab ṕıa Conċoboṕ ı Calcen ṕo abnaċca, .ı. Ollam Póċla ⁊ moṕṕeṕṕıuṕ leıṕṕ bıa maccaıb, ⁊ bıa uıb, ⁊ co n-bṕéım aıle bo maċıb Ulab. Uaıṕlı Cuaċe be Dananb ıṕ ın bṕuʒ. (.ı. cen moċa moṕṕeṕṕıuṕ ṕo abnaċc bıb h-ı Calcın).ı. Luʒ ocuṕ Óe mac Olloman, ocuṕ Oʒma, ocuṕ Caıṕṕṕı mac Ecaıne (.ı. ban ṕılı) ocuṕ Ecaın ṕeın, ocuṕ ın Daʒba, ocuṕ a cṕı meıc (.ı. Aeb, ocuṕ Oenʒuṕ ocuṕ Ceṕmaıc) ocuṕ ṕóċaıbe móṕ aṕ ċena bo Cuaıċ De Dananb, ocuṕ Peṕ m-bolʒ, ocuṕ caıċ aṕ ċena.—*Leabhar na h-Uidhri*, p. 38, col. 2.

" The chiefs of Ulster before Conchobhor were buried at Taillten, viz. Ollamh Fodhla, and seven of his sons, and grandsons, with others of the chiefs of Ulster. The nobles of the Tuatha de Danan (with the exception of seven of them who were interred at Taillten), were buried at Brugh, i. e. Lug, and Oe, son of Olloman, and Ogma, and Cairpri, son of Etain (i. e. the poetess) and Etain herself, and the Dagdai and his three sons (i. e. Aedh and Oengus, and Cermait) and a great number besides of the Tuatha De Danann and of the Ferbolgs and of other persons also."— *Leabhar na h-Uidhri*, p. 38, col. 2.

From this it would appear that, in addition to the Ultonians being buried at Taillten, seven of the Tuatha de Danann dynasty, whose names are given above, were also interred here.

On the next page of our valuable old MS., alluding to the ancient fairs held at the cemeteries, we have the following poetical enumeration of the mounds, carns, or tombs to be found at each of the three cemeteries above referred to:—

Cóeca cnoc ın ceó Oenuó bıb ṗın ;
Coeca cnoc, ém, ın Oenaó Cṗuaóan,
Ocuṗ coeca cnoc ın Oenuó Calcen,
Ocuṗ coeca ın Oenuó ın bṗoᵹa.
Leabhar na h- Uidri p. 39, col. 1, top.

" Fifty hills in each Oenach of them :
Fifty hills at Oenach Cruachan,
And fifty hills at Oenach Taillten,
And fifty [hills] at Oenach in Broga."
Leabhar na h- Uidhri, p. 39, col. 1, top.

The ruins or sites of more than half the above number of carns set down as being at Taillten can still be pointed out on the Loughcrew Hills.

Out of the list of the ancient Royal Cemeteries of Ireland before given, the sites of two only, viz. Croghan, about the middle of the county Roscommon, and Brugh, in Meath, a few miles west of Drogheda, are definitely known. The sites of the remainder, so far as we know, have yet to be established.

In the preceding extracts, from the most ancient MS. we possess, we have so much definite information given as to that of Taillten, that it appears to us almost impossible to doubt its existence on the Loughcrew Hills. If Taillte was buried here, in whose memory the fair and games of Taillten were established by Lugh Lamhfhada, whose death is recorded at B. C. 1829, it must have been used as a cemetery for upwards of 18 centuries before the Christian era; but, if we only date its being used from the time of the name of the first on the list mentioned as interred here, viz. Ollamh Fodhla, whose death is set down by The Four Masters as having occurred B. c. 1277, it must be thirty-one centuries and a half old.

As to the period at which the cemetery of Taillten ceased to be used as such, it is here distinctly stated that it was used by the Ultonians up to the time of Conchobhor, who specified his wish to be buried elsewhere. Now, as Conchobhor is set down in the generally received correct Annals of Tigherneach* as having died A. D. 33, and Ollamh Fodhla by the Four Masters at B. c. 1277, it is plain that the cemetery of Taillten must have been in actual use at least for nearly thirteen centuries before the Christian era, when, on the death of Conchobhor, it ceased to be used.

As Conchobhor and Crimthann were the two kings of the two great dynasties reigning in Ireland at the commencement of the Christian period, and Crimthann being the first of his line, according to *Senchas na Relec*, buried at Brugh, we have a very clear view, as Mr. Fergusson† points out, of the relative age and history of the two Royal

---

* Pronounced *Teerna.*
† " Rude Stone Monuments," p. 221.

Cemeteries of Meath. In fact, it was not until Taillten was abandoned
that the kings began to bury at Brugh, in the neighbourhood of
Drogheda.

In the poem before quoted there is an epithet applied to the cemetery of Taillten which strikes us as very remarkable. The line
runs :—

" The Cemetery of Taillten, *the select.*"

Now, we think the epithet here applied to Taillten will throw
some light on the cause of the Ulster kings and chiefs coming so far,
all the way from Emania, beside the present city of Armagh, to bury
their dead at Taillten; for, probably, in the whole island there could
not be found a more *select* and remarkable site than our ancient kings
fixed upon when they adopted the heights of that range of hills we
now call Sliabh na Caillighe for their future cemetery.

From them the mountains overhanging the bays of Carlingford and
Sligo are visible, thus giving a telescopic view of Ireland from coast to
coast at the narrowest part of the island. Moreover, persons well
acquainted with the general face of the country are accustomed to point
out, from the peaks of Sliabh na Caillighe, with the aid, of course, of a
clear atmosphere, elevations in eighteen out of the thirty-two counties
in Ireland! This ceases to surprise us when we recollect that the
square-root of once and a half the height in feet of any elevation on
the globe's surface is equal to the distance of the offing, or sensible
horizon, in miles : hence, the highest peak of Sliabh na Caillighe,
having an altitude of 904 feet, must command a view of, at least, 37
miles all around, in a perfectly clear horizon ; and atmospheric re-
fraction will increase this distance by about three miles.

Now, taking Sliabh na Caillighe as a centre, and with a radius of 40
miles, sweeping a circle on the map of Ireland, we find that this circle
will include the counties of Meath, Westmeath, Longford, Cavan, and
Monaghan; the greater portions of Dublin, Kildare, King's County, Roscommon, Leitrim, Fermanagh, Armagh, and Louth ; and will include
small portions, or very nearly touch the confines, of Wicklow, Queen's
County, Galway, Sligo, Tyrone, and Down. Following out the same
process of calculation, any mountain attaining the height of 2000 feet,
under favourable circumstances, might be visible from Sliabh na Caillighe, if not more than 92 miles distant; and this would include every
mountain of 2000 feet and upwards in height in every county in Ireland, except in Cork and Kerry.

When the sun shines out resplendently over these hills, chasing
away the gloom of darkness which occasionally, and often very sud-
denly, obscures their summits, the gorgeous panorama, displaying a
profuse wealth of natural attractions, is seen with great distinctness of
outline, and presents a prospect probably one of the most diversified
and beautiful in the whole island. Nature seems to have lavished her
choicest treasures upon the scene, and the magnificent combination of
receding eminences, and distant lakes, and gracefully undulating
plains, could not fail to quicken the imagination to a profound sense

of solemn grandeur.* What wonder, then, that one old bardic chronicler, as we have seen, should have called this place " the *fair-hilled* Taillten," and that another should have described it as " The cemetery of Taillten, *the select*"?

No wonder that the great Ultonian kings and chiefs, and other kings and celebrities, at whatever distance they may have usually resided, should have yearned to make this spot their last resting place. Indeed, to us the only wonder is, that so remarkable a site for a cemetery should have been ever abandoned, so long as pagan sepulture was practised in the country.

From the accompanying Map the distribution and relative sites of the still-remaining carns can be best studied. Under the nomenclature of the letters of the alphabet each carn has already been summarily described by us, on 26th February, 1866, and published in the Proceedings of the Royal Irish Academy, Vol. IX., p. 355, &c., to which, or to the subjoined Appendix, reference can be made for further details.

Looking at this map of the carns, one cannot but be struck with

---

* In addition to what nature has done to lay the foundation of scenic beauty in this district, it is but justice to record that much of the picturesque effect, looking westwards, is essentially due to the critical judgment and refined artistic taste with which, during a long life, the late James Lenox William Naper, Esq., directed and superintended the various improvements carried out upon his extensive estate. His benevolent disposition and his genuine kindness of heart induced him, with the exception of occasional short absences, to spend his useful life upon his own property, almost daily devising plans for adding to the comforts of his poorer class of tenantry ; but, above all, feeling and taking the deepest practical interest in the successful working of the excellent schools upon his property, as he believed them to be the most effective engines for promoting social progress, with certainty and permanency, in the humbler ranks of life. The following incident may be worth recording, as it affords an explanation of the origin of some of the charming views about Loughcrew.

From the opening of the singularly successful schools in Oldcastle,[a] founded and endowed under the will of a native of the town, Laurence Gilson, whose death took place on 14th April, 1810, the late J. L. W. Naper, Esq., acted as chairman of the board of trustees by whom the schools are managed; and, up to the period of his death, on 2nd September, 1868, uniformly took a deep interest in watching over their efficient working. The annual public examination of the schools was fixed for Tuesday, 9th June, 1868, while the writer, who acted as Inspector of the schools for the trustees, was one of an antiquarian party on a visit to Loughcrew. On that morning, while pacing about in front of Loughcrew House with Mr. Naper, who was awaiting the coming round of his carriage to proceed to the examination, the writer happened to remark, while looking in the direction of Lough Sheelin—" What a picturesque scene !" This accidental observation appeared to amuse him ; and he then stated that, after the site for the house had been fixed upon, he, standing where we then stood, sketched the outline of the undulating country in front, in all its arid bareness of character ; and, having afterwards in his studio worked up this outline *into a picture* to please himself, he planted here and there accordingly, leaving some hill tops bare, others crowned with wood, and, in the whole, producing the present exquisite panoramic view, which he lived to the good old age of seventy-six to enjoy from the front of Loughcrew House.

[a] During the year 1871, of the children of the town and neighbourhood receiving an excellent free education, in addition to being gratuitously supplied with all necessary books and school requisites, there was an average of 645·3 pupils on the rolls of the three schools (Boys', Girls', and Infants') in the Institution ; and, on an average, there were 372·7 of these pupils in actual daily attendance throughout the year.

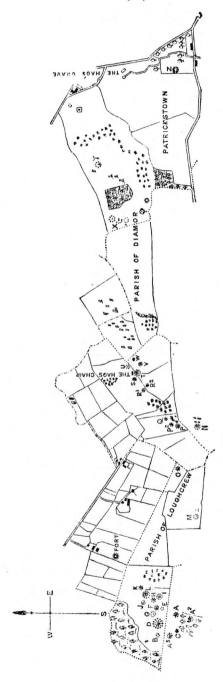

Map of the Remains of the ancient Royal Cemetery of Tailiten,
on the Loughcrew Hills, Oldcastle, Co. Meath, Ireland.
Scale : 2·64 inches to a Statute Mile.

the general arrangement of them into groups, the central one of each group being much larger than the surrounding ones; which naturally leads to the inference that each group may represent a dynasty, the central carn being probably the tomb of the founder.

It would be reasonable to suppose that Queen Taillte's last resting-place should be found in the cemetery named after her ; but we have been unable, so far as our present investigations have gone, to point to any one of the carns as Taillte's tomb, although we strongly suspect that the large carn on the peak now called the hill of Patrickstown, the stones constituting which have been nearly all carted away for the purpose of building adjoining fences, was such ; for there are many still living who describe this carn, before its recent destruction, as the most conspicuous of all upon the hills, particularly when viewed from the great rath at Telltown, the probable site of one of her principal residences, as we have before seen. Had this carn been situated on Mr. Naper's property it would in all likelihood have escaped desecration and destruction.

Having learned, from the extracts above quoted, the names of some of those who were buried at the ancient cemetery of Taillten, it becomes legitimate for us to inquire, if, among these remains, there be any positive or distinctive peculiarities by which they could be indicatively associated with the memory of any of those stated in the foregoing extracts to have been buried at Taillten. It will be seen that the first mentioned as interred at Taillten was Ollamh Fodhla,* the great law-giver

---

* Pronounced *Ollăv Fōla :* i. e. the Ollamh, or chief Poet of Fodhla, or Ireland. We are indebted to Dr. O'Donovan's translation of the Annals of Ireland for the following particulars, and the valuable notes thereon by the learned editor. It will be necessary to keep in mind, in reading them, that the Chronology adopted by the Four Masters, following the computation of the Septuagint, as given by St. Jerome in his edition of the Chronicon of Eusebius, makes the first year of our era agree with the year of the world, 5199.

" The Age of the world, 3847. After Sedna had been five years in the sovereignty, he fell by Fiacha Finscothach and Muineamhon, son of Cas Clothach, at Cruachain."[a]

" The Age of the World, 3848. The first year of the reign of Fiacha Finscothach over Ireland."

" The Age of the world, 3867. After Fiacha Finscothach had been twenty years in the sovereignty of Ireland he fell by Muineamhon, son of Cas. Every plain in Ireland abounded with flowers and shamrocks in the time of Fiacha. These flowers, moreover, were found full of wine, so that the wine was squeezed into bright vessels. Wherefore, the cognomen, Fiacha Fin-scothach,[b] continued to be applied to him."

" The Age of the World, 3868. This was the first year of the reign of Muineamhon, son of Cas Clothach, over Ireland."

" The Age of the World, 3872. At the end of the fifth year of Muineamhon, he died of the plague in Magh-Aidhne.[c] It was Muineamhon that first caused

---

[a] *Cruachain.* Now Rathcroghan, near Belanagare, in the county of Roscommon.

[b] *Fin-scothach:* i. e. of the Wine-flowers. Keating gives this cognomen the same interpretation, but in Connell Mageoghegan's translation of the Annals of Clonmacnois, it is stated that this King " was surnamed Ffinnsgohagh of the abundance of *white flowers* that were in his time," which seems more probable, as wine was then unknown in Ireland.

[c] *Magh-Aidhne:* a level district in the present county of Galway, all comprised in the diocese of Kilmacduagh.

of Ireland, upwards of seven hundred years before Solon* legislated for Greece ; and on the highest peak of a range of hills, rendered the more conspicuous and remarkable because they are the highest in the com-

---

chains of gold[d] (to be worn) on the necks of kings and chieftains in Ireland."

"The Age of the World, 3873.   The first year of Faildeargdoid."

"The Age of the World, 3882.   After Faildeargdoid had been ten years in the sovereignty, he fell by Ollamh Fodhla, son of Fiacha Finscothach, in the battle of Teamhair.   It was by the King Faildeargdoid[e] that gold rings were first worn upon the hands of chieftains in Ireland."

"The Age of the World, 3883.   The first year of the reign of Ollamh Fodhla, son of Fiacha Finscothach."

"The Age of the World, 3922.   Ollamh Fodhla, after having been forty years in the sovereignty of Ireland, died at his own *mur* (house), at Teamhair.[f]   He was the first king by whom the Feis-Teamhrach[g] was established ; and it was by him Mur-Ollamhan was erected at Teamhair.   It was he also that appointed a chieftain over every cantred,[h] and a Brughaidh over every townland, who were all to serve the king of Ireland.[i]   Eochaidh was the first name of Ollamh Fodhla ; and he was called Ollamh (Fodhla) because he had been first a learned Ollamh, and afterwards king of (Fodhla, i. e. of) Ireland."

"The Age of the World, 3923.   This was the first year of the reign of Finnachta, son of Ollamh Fodhla, over Ireland."

"The Age of the World, 3942.   This was the twentieth year of the reign of Finnachta over Ireland.   He afterwards died of the plague in Magh-inis, in Uladh.[j]   It was in the reign of Finnachta that snow fell with the taste of wine, which blackened the grass.   From this the cognomen Finnachta,[k] adhered to him. Elim was his name at first."

---

[d] *Chains of gold.* Keating has the same, and in Mageoghegan's Annals of Clonmacnois it is expressed as follows :—"Mownemon was the first King that devised gould to be wrought in chains fit to be wore about men's necks, and rings to be put on their fingers, which was" (were) "then in great use."

[e] *Faildeargdoid.* He is called Alldeargoid by Keating, and Aldergoid in the Annals of Clonmacnois.   This name is derived from ꝝail, a ring ; ꝺeaꝼᵹ, red ; and ꝺoiꝺ, the hand. " In his time gold rings were much used on men and women's fingers in this Realm." *Annals of Clonmacnois.*

[f] *His own mur at Teamhair :* i. e., Mur-Ollamhan, i. e. Ollamh Fodhla's house at Tara.   In Mageoghegan's translation of the Annals of Clonmacnois it is stated "that he builded a fair palace at Taragh only for the learned sort of this realm, to dwell in at his own charges."   But this is probably one of Mageoghegan's interpolations.   A similar explanation of Mur-Ollamhan is given by O'Flaherty in his *Ogygia*, p. 214 ; but Keating, who quotes an ancient poem as authority for the triennial feast or meeting at Tara, has not a word about the palace built for the Ollamhs.   *See Petrie's Antiquities of Tara Hill*, p. 6.

[g] *Feis-Teamhrach.* This term is translated " Temorensia Comitia," by Dr. Lynch, in *Cambrensis Eversus*, pp. 59, 60, 301, and by O'Flaherty, in *Ogygia*, part III., c. 29 ; but it is called " Cena" (Coena) " Teamra," in the Annals of Tighernach, at the year 461, and translated Feast of Taragh by Mageoghegan, in his version of the Annals of Clonmacnois, in which the following notice of it occurs :—" Ollow Fodla, of the house of Ulster, was King of Ireland, and of him Ulster took the name.   He was the first King of this land that ever kept the great Feast at Taragh, which feast was kept once a year, whereunto all the King's friends and dutiful subjects came yearly ; and such as came not were taken for the King's enemies, and to be prosecuted by the law and sword, as undutiful to the State."

[h] *Cantred :* cꝛioꝺa ceꝺ : i. e. a hundred or barony containing one hundred and twenty quarters of land. It is translated " cantaredus or centivillaria regio" by Colgan. *Trias Thaum.*, p. 19, in. 51.

[i] *A brughaidh over every townland.* Dr. Lynch renders this passage "singulis agrorum tricenariis Dynastam, singulis Burgis præfectum constituit." A brughaidh, among the ancient Irish, meant a farmer ; and his ꝃaile or townland comprised four quarters, or four hundred and eighty large Irish acres of land.

[j] *Magh-inis in Uladh.* Now the barony of Lecale, in the county of Down.

[k] *Finnachta.* Keating gives a similar interpretation ; but it is evidently legendary, because Finnachta, or Finnshneachta, was very common as the name of a man among the ancient Irish, denoting *Niveus*, or snow-white. The name is still preserved in the surname O'Finneachta, *anglicè* Finaghty.

paratively flat county of Meath, we still have, among the general
destruction which has befallen the others around it, as well as the
partial injury to itself, a very perfect carn,† with an unique stone
chair placed in its northern boundary.

"The Hag's Chair," 18th September, 1865.

This great stone seat has been in latter times only known by the
name of "The Hag's Chair"; and we have given this name to it on
the map, with the view of its being easily found by the archæological
tourist. In order to give an idea of the state in which we found it,
immediately before we commenced to clear away the earth and stones
from about it, thus revealing its inscribed characters, from a photograph taken by Charles W. Hamilton, Esq., we here present, arrayed
in its lichen garb, and just as it then appeared, a very correct engraving
of it.

"The Age of the World, 3943. The first year of the reign of Slanoll,[1] son of
Ollamh Fodhla, over Ireland."

"The Age of the World, 3959. The seventeenth year of Slanoll in the
sovereignty; and he died, at the end of that time, at Teamhair [Tara], and it is not
known what disease carried him off; he was found dead, but his colour did not
change. He was afterwards buried; and after his body had been forty years
in the grave, it was taken up by his son, i. e., Oilioll mac Slanuill; and the body
had remained without rotting or decomposing during this period. This thing was
a great wonder and surprise to the men of Ireland."

For further particulars as to the reigns of the descendants of Ollamh Fodhla,
see "Annals of Ireland by the Four Masters," Vol. I. p. 55, &c.

* Solon, one of the seven sages of Greece and the great Athenian legislator, is
recorded to have died B. C. 558; and Ollamh Fodhla B. C. 1277.

† See Map, Carn T.

[1] *Slanoll.* Keating derives this name from ſlán, health; and oll, great; and adds that
he was so called because all his subjects enjoyed great health in his time. The Annals of Clonmacnois contain the same remark:—"During whose reign the kingdom was free from all
manner of sickness:" and add:—"It is unknown to any of what he died, but died quietly on
his bed; and after that his body remained *five* years buried, and did not rott, consume, or
change collour. He reigned 26 years."

D

As we know that such seats, in a state of primitive civilization, were used for purposes of inauguration and the administration of pristine laws, we can have little difficulty in associating this chair with the memory of some one laid here to his rest who, during his lifetime, must have been in a remarkable degree connected either with the making or the administration, or both, of the laws of the country.

And to whom, keeping in view the preceding MS. testimony, could this great megalithic chair be more appropriately ascribed than to Ollamh Fodhla? It would be natural to suppose that for the site of the tomb of the great King and law-maker, his posterity (or, indeed, probably he himself, during his own lifetime), selected the most elevated spot on the entire range; hence, we propose to call the carn on that spot, 904 feet above the sea level, and situated on the middle hill, Ollamh Fodhla's Tomb; the great stone seat Ollamh Fodhla's Chair; and the ruined remains of the smaller surrounding carns, six of which still remain, the tombs of his sons and grandsons, mentioned in the previous extracts. In fact, on the summit of the highest hill in the site of this ancient royal cemetery, we believe there still exist the remains of the tombs of the dynasty of Ollamh Fodhla.

Richard Rolt Brash, Esq., C. E., M. R. I. A., in an article in the "Gentleman's Magazine," for April, 1865, "On Ancient Chairs and Stones of Inauguration," says:—

"The class of monument now under consideration has been found in countries widely apart. Examples of the stone chair in its most ancient types have been met with in Ireland, Wales, Greece, and South America. From the remotest historic times the chair has been associated with the ideas of power, sovereignty, and dignity. The exhumed sculptures of ancient Nineveh represent her monarchs on chairs, and divinities borne in procession seated on the same. The great statue of Jupiter, by Phidias, was seated in a chair of ivory. The Jupiter Optimus Maximus of the Romans was seated in a curule chair in his temple on the Capitoline hill. With us the seat of royal dignity is associated with, or stands for, the sovereignty of states and kingdoms. Thus we speak of the thrones of England, France, or Russia. In this sense it also stands for high academical attainments and offices; thus we speak of the chairs of history, of philosophy, of science, of poetry, &c. No doubt in semi-barbarous times the rude chair of stone was also associated with similar ideas. Upon it the ancient kings and toparchs were inaugurated with rude but impressive ceremonies, and from it the chief, judge, or law-giver dispensed justice.

"The place selected for the ceremonies of inauguration was usually a natural or artificial eminence in the centre of a large *magh* (field) or plain. The elected chief occupied either a stone chair, or stood upon a flat stone sacred to the purpose, and called Leac-na-Righ, 'the flag or stone of the kings,' and which was preserved for centuries, and regarded as the palladium of the state."

After this follows an interesting account of the vicissitudes of the coronation chair of the O'Neills of Clandeboy, which for ages stood on the hill of Castlereagh, the inauguration place of the chiefs of that race, about two miles from Belfast, now preserved at Rathcarrick, Co. Sligo; and also of the destruction in the month of August, 1602, of the inauguration stone-chair of the elder branch of the O'Neills at Tullahogue, near Dungannon, Co. Tyrone; as well as of the fate of the inauguration stone of the O'Donnells, which, after being removed from its original site on the rock or hill of Doune, lay in the ruined chancel of the neighbouring ancient church of Kilmacrenan, Co. Donegal, until about 50 years ago, when it was either stolen or destroyed.

What first led us to conceive the idea that this carn must be the tomb of Ollamh Fodhla was the fact of its having, as one of the thirty-seven large stones in the periphery of its base, a great stone-chair facing the north, in our days popularly called "The Hag's Chair," measuring 10 feet in breadth, 6 feet high, and 2 feet thick; from which dimensions it must be upwards of ten tons in weight, allowing twelve cubic feet of rock to weigh one ton. It occurred to us that, instead of this being the chair of any old hag of antiquity, whether real or mythical, it would be much more reasonable to look upon it as having had, in the long past days of its glory, some practical use.

At that remote period in the history of man, before the advent of Christianity, it is well known that the sun was an object of worship; and the very fact that the entrances to the interior chambers of the majority of the carns on the Loughcrew Hills point to the east, or the rising sun, bears strong internal evidence that this form of worship prevailed when these tombs or carns were constructed. If such were the case, for we are without any absolute historic evidence on the point, we can well imagine how appropriately a great seat of justice was placed in the north side of the great law-maker's tomb, from which, with all the solemnity attaching to the place, his laws were administered, say at mid-day, with the recipients of the adjudication fully confronted with the great luminary, the object of their worship. For these reasons we propose, henceforth, to call this remarkable stone chair, emblazoned as it is, both on front and back, with characters at present perfectly unintelligible to us, "Ollamh Fodhla's Chair."

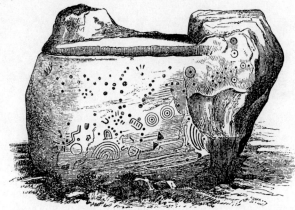

Ollamh Fodhla's Chair (Front View).

Unfortunately, from a natural fracture in the stone, a considerable portion of the back has scaled off, and the pieces being lost, we are now unable even to guess what cryptic characters may have been inscribed upon the lost portions. In the following woodcut, however, it will be seen that the portion of the original back its remaining, is inscribed with characters quite analogous with those upon its front.

The chair is a rock of native Lower Silurian grit, having a rude seat hollowed out of the centre, and leaving an elevation at each side of about nine inches above the seat, the back having now fallen away.

Ollamh Fodhla's Chair (Back View).

The apparent cross carved into the centre of the seat, as well as two others on adjoining marginal upright stones, are not to be mistaken for characters of ancient date, as they were cut for trigonometrical purposes in the year 1836, by the men then encamped on Sliabh na Caillighe, and engaged in the triangulation survey of the country under Captain Stotherd and Lieutenants Greatorex and Chaytor, R. E.

If, then, it can be satisfactorily concluded that this carn is the

The Tomb of Ollamh Fodhla.

tomb of Ollamh Fodhla, the internal evidence for which being the sculptured stone-chair, or judicial seat, the question is settled ; and all doubt as to the identification of the ancient cemetery, whose name and history had become lost in the various changes and troubles through which the country passed during the long lapse of upwards of 3,000 years, from the days of Ollamh Fodhla to our own time, must at once disappear. We may, indeed, fairly conclude that we have disin-tombed from the relics of time the last resting-place of one who, in this island, was a great pioneer in the civilization of his fellow-men at a period when the actions of the human race, in most other parts of the world, were probably governed by no better laws than the impulses of animal passion, dictated on the spur of the moment.

The preceding view, from a slightly north-westerly aspect, is engraved from a photograph taken by Charles William Hamilton, Esq., in September, 1865, while the original explorations were in progress. The upright stones seen on the left must not be mistaken as belonging to Ollamh Fodhla's tomb, being the boundary stones of the remains of an adjoining carn.

The original shape of this carn still remains comparatively perfect,

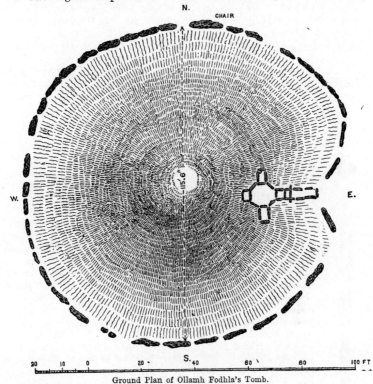

Ground Plan of Ollamh Fodhla's Tomb.

consisting of a conical mound of loose stones, nearly all apparently fragments of the native rock, Lower Silurian grit. It is thirty-eight and one-half yards in diameter at the base, having an elevation of twenty-one paces in slant-height from base to summit. A retaining wall, consisting of thirty-seven large flags laid on edge, and varying in length from six to twelve feet, surrounds the base externally; and, on the eastern side, this surrounding circle of large stones curves inwards for a distance of eight or nine yards on each side of a point where the passage to the interior chambers commences, the bearing of the passage being E. 10° S., probably intended to face the rising sun at that period of the year when the occupant of the tomb was laid to his rest, or when the fabrication of the carn was commenced. The peculiarities of construction and the internal arrangements of the chambers will be better understood from the foregoing.

Inside the retaining wall of large flag stones, as far as was examined, and, apparently, going all round the base of the carn, was piled up a layer, rising from three to four feet in height, and about two feet in thickness, of broken lumps of sparkling native Irish quartz, a rock which does not geologically belong to this part of the island ; and which, consequently, must have found its way from some distant locality. The nearest native beds of quartz rock are to be met with at Howth, about fifty miles S. E. from Sliabh na Caillighe ; in Wicklow, sixty miles, S. E. ; in Donegal, ninety miles, N. ; in Sligo, about the same distance, N. W. ; in Galway, 110 miles, W. ; but the fragments used here may, probably, have been obtained on the spot from some glacial deposits from Donegal, without actually transporting them from any of the localities above mentioned.

In the rifled state in which the interior of this carn was found by us, during our explorations, in 1865, the entrance to the passage was closed by two irregular blocks of stone ; and in the commencement of the passage were dropped three large boulders, completely filling up the first chamber in the passage to the height of about twenty inches, and for six feet in length, up to the first stone standing across the passage, and as far as the only remaining roofing stone over it. These three rude boulders rested upon two flooring flags in the passage, underneath which, when raised, was found a layer of very small stones of different kinds, and chips of quartz. Among these loose stones on the bottom of the passage were deposited fragments of bones, some pieces of which appeared to be portions of a human skull, and four large molar teeth, either of a horse or an ox. Although the general outline of the carn still remains in its original state, the roofing stones covering the passage, with one exception, No. 26, which is six feet in length and eighteen inches in breadth and thickness, resting across the third pair of uprights, have all long since disappeared, as well as the greater portion of the roofing stones which formerly covered the central octagonal chamber. At present there are only about thirty overlapping roofing stones remaining *in situ*, carrying the roof over the central chamber to a height of about ten feet.

The first operation in the examination of this carn, in September, 1865, was to remove the loose stones which, in the vandalism of taking away the roofing stones at some former period, had fallen in and filled up the passage and chambers. Three large bones, probably belonging to a deer, were found among the loose stones which filled up the central chamber ; and near the bottom, among these stones, and close to the entrance to the north-

A

B

C

D

E
Bronze Pin.

ern chamber, a bronze pin, 2⅝ inches in length, here represented full size, was found. It is beautifully incrusted with that patina, or green enamel, peculiar to bronze, and appears to have been much worn. The ornamentation on the head is shown at A. The stem, which also contains traces of ornamentation between B and C, is round from B to D, swelling to C and then contracting to D, where it begins to change into a four flat-sided point, thick below D, and tapering down to E. Although this pin must be classed with objects of ancient Irish art, it is not probable, from its being picked up among the loose stones, where it may have found its way by accident, that it can lay claim to anything like the antiquity of the tomb itself. It is here given simply as having been found in this ancient carn, without suggesting any period as to its own age.

The central chamber was floored or closely covered by five thin flags, underneath which, on being raised, were found fragments of charred bones, and small splintered stones, mixed with pieces of charcoal.

The interior of this carn had been so well plundered at some former period that no remains of the actual mode of sepulture were found in it ; but, judging from the quantities of charred human bones, broken urns, inscribed bone flakes, polished stone balls, articles of bronze and iron, bone, glass and amber beads, &c.,* collected from the other carns during our examination of them in September, 1865, two important facts would appear to be clearly established therefrom, viz., that cremation of the dead was practised on Sliabh na Caillighe up to the Christian era, at the commencement of which, as previously shown, the use of this cemetery was given up ; and that, during the period the cemetery was in actual use, the people must have been acquainted with the use of articles made not only of stone and of bronze, but of iron, glass, amber, and bone.

If, however, nothing has come down to us immediately associated with the remains of the original interment in this carn, future history may have something far more interesting to record, when some successful student in archaic sculptures shall have been fortunate enough to discover the key for interpreting the meaning, whether ideographic or symbolic, or merely ornamental, intended to be conveyed by the curious, and at present mystic, characters inscribed upon the stones forming the interior chambers. There is little doubt that, should one of the old sculptors of these devices, by any possibility be able once more to "revisit the glimpses of the moon," and be confronted with an inscription on one of our modern sepulchral monuments, the reading of which to us is so plain and simple, and so conformable with the science of grammar, he would be as much puzzled, probably more so, to make sense or meaning out of our characters, as we are to-day out of his !

A basaltic slab, not three feet square, turned up near Rosetta, on the western mouth of the Nile, by a French officer of Engineers in the month of August, 1799, at present preserved in the British

---

* See Proceedings of R. I. A., Vol. IX., p. 355, &c., or Appendix, p. 51, &c.

Museum, and now commonly known as "The Rosetta Stone," has, from its fruitful contents, led to the deciphering and reading of what had then become mystic characters on the pyramids of Egypt; and, if we doubt the possibility of such another lucky accident leading to the interpretation of the characters on the inscribed stones in this and the adjoining carns, as well as analogously inscribed stones in carns in other countries, may we not at least reasonably hope that by collecting them, and closely analysing and comparing the analogies of the characters, the mystery of which is at present impenetrable to us, every line, and cup, and curve, and figure on these monuments of the past, will assume a definite and distinct meaning? But it, unfortunately, too frequently happens in our days that those who wish to prosecute such studies want the necessary time and leisure to do it; and those, upon the other hand, who possess both the opportunity and the ability, do not want to do it. It would be idle to suppose, as some have done, that these markings are nothing more than childish amusements. The forms and the arrangements of many of them appear to indicate a symbolic character, and thus refute the idea of their being intended, as others assert, for mere ornamentation.

Judging from the memorials of the past which have come down to us, there appears to have been at all times, and, indeed, in every country, even before the invention of letters, a craving in the human breast, just as we find it to be the case in our own days, to perpetuate memories. Should we hope, in the slow school of archæology, hereafter to be able to unravel the meaning of the inscribed records of the age of stone-literature, if we may be allowed the use of such an expression in reference to ancient rock-markings, we must for the present be satisfied to accumulate these characters largely, even without understanding them, or too closely investigating their meaning; and, when the number of these collected elements shall be found sufficient, then some future student of archæology will, undoubtedly, be able, by careful analogies and comparisons, to render the solution of their meaning not only possible but practicable, from the consideration of these assembled elements. The following inscriptions on the stones in Ollamh Fodhla's tomb are here given, in the fullest confidence that this hope will soon be realized.

With each stone numbered for reference in the descriptions which are to follow, we submit a ground plan of the interior of Ollamh Fodhla's tomb (see next page).

The long passage and the tricameral arrangement round a central octagonal chamber give the general outline the appearance of a cross, which shape, judging from the internal arrangements in most of the other carns on Sliabh na Caillighe, as well as at New Grange and Dowth, in the same county, appears to have been the favourite form adopted by our pagan ancestors in the construction of the tombs of their great people.

The passage has an average breadth of three feet, and is seventeen feet in length; while the distance from the commencement of the passage to the farthest extremity of the opposite chamber is twenty-

eight feet. The distance from the back of the southern to that of the
northern chamber is sixteen feet four inches, the distance between
their entrances being seven feet; while the distance from the termination of the passage to the entrance of the opposite or western chamber

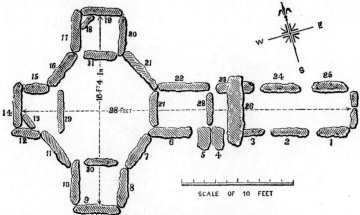

Ground Plan of the Interior of Ollamh Fodhla's Tomb.

measures six feet three inches. In fact, the central octagonal chamber may be said to be about seven feet wide in every direction.

The execution of the devices in this carn appears to be almost
entirely in *punched* work, while there are examples of characters either

No. 1.

engraved or rubbed into the stone; but, whether or not by a metallic
tool, would now be difficult to decide.

Believing that giving to the public a faithful transcript of the
characters inscribed upon the interior chamber-stones in this carn will
be the surest means of leading to their interpretation, we submit, from

careful drawings of the stones, engravings of these devices, in the following order, beginning with the first stone on the left hand side as you enter the passage.

No. 1 sinks out of sight below a horizontal flooring slab, but the portion visible measures 3 feet 6 inches in height, 2 feet 3 inches in breadth, and six inches in thickness. Over a very curious wheel-

No. 2.

shaped figure, occupying the lower surface of the stone, and measuring 14 inches across, the prevailing character of the sculpture will be seen to be cup-and-circle-marking of various forms.

Nos. 4 and 5.

The measurements of No. 2 are four and a half feet in height, three feet four inches broad, and four inches thick. It will be remarked that the sculptures occupy principally the upper half of the stone.

No. 3, the third stone on the southern side of the passage, is four feet high, two feet wide, and six inches thick, having no sculptured markings now discernible upon it.

Each of the stones, numbered 4 and 5, stands four feet in height, presents a front surface of one foot in breadth, and recedes backwards for two feet nine inches. Standing compactly together as they do, they are so represented here.

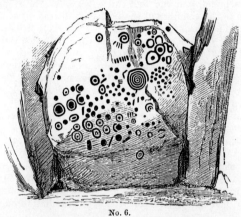

No. 6.

This, No. 6, is the terminal stone on the southern side of the passage, and measures four feet nine inches in height, three feet five inches in breadth, and is nine inches thick.

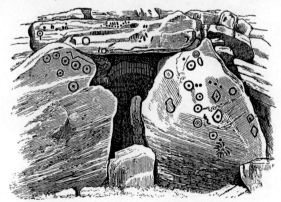

Nos. 7, 30, 11, and lintel.

The breadth of the passage at its termination and the entrance into the central octagonal chamber, off which are three quadrilateral chambers, constituting the arms and top of the cruciform figure which forms the interior plan of the tomb, is only three feet one inch.

The entrance to the southern chamber is here represented, giving a view of the sculptures upon the stones Nos. 7 and 11, as well as upon the lintel stone over them. No. 7, on the left, measures five feet in height, three feet two inches in width, and one foot in thickness: No. 11, on the right, measures five feet two inches in height, four feet four inches in width, and one foot in thickness: and the lintel stone over the entrance is four feet eight inches long, one foot seven inches broad, and one foot thick. No. 30, the stone closing in the entrance to the chamber at the bottom is devoid of sculpture, and measures one foot eight inches in height, the same in breadth, and is six inches thick, leaving an opening over it, or entrance into the chamber, of upwards of three feet in height.

It is deserving of notice that several of the lines upon the lintel stone have been supposed by some to be Ogham marks; but they have been examined in our presence by the Right Rev. Charles Graves, D. D., Bishop of Limerick, who has so successfully made this occult mode of writing one of the special studies of his life, and they have been pronounced by him not to be Ogham.

The southern chamber is nearly four feet square, and is covered by a horizontal roofing flag. When the loose stones which had fallen in, by the former uncovering of the central chamber, had been removed, the earth on the floor was found mixed with splinters of burned bones. No other indications of burial were found, showing the state in which the chamber had been left, after some unrecorded plundering of its contents.

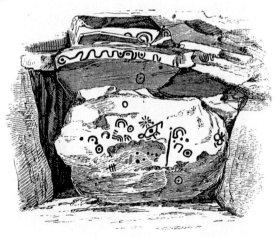

No. 8.

The characters on the first stone on the left, after entering, are here represented; the stone itself measuring three feet seven inches in height, four feet in breadth, and six inches in thickness. Projecting slightly over No. 8 will be observed the ends of two other inscribed stones, from which it is evident, as the devices pass out of sight into the structure, that they were sculptured before their erection in their present position.

This stone is opposite to the entrance, and forms the southern wall

No. 9.

of the chamber. It is four feet five inches high, three feet wide, and nine inches thick.

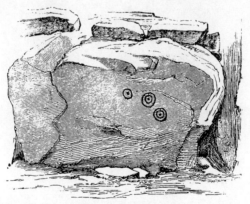

No. 10.

The western wall of the southern chamber is formed by the stone here represented, measuring three feet four inches high, three feet ten inches wide, and nine inches thick.

The entrance to the western chamber, opposite the passage from the exterior, and forming the top of the cruciform figure represented

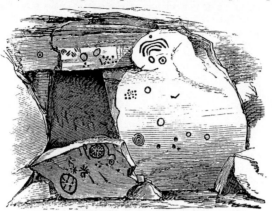

Nos. 29, 16, and lintel.

in the ground plan of the tomb, is here shown. The upright on the left has been already described as No. 11; that on the right, No. 16, measures five feet two inches in height, is four feet wide, and nine inches thick. The stone closing the entrance to the chamber at the bottom, No. 29, measures two feet nine inches in length, two feet four inches

Roofing stone over western chamber.

in height, and is five inches thick. Unfortunately, the lintel over the entrance has become cracked across, and has sunk considerably since the chamber below it was freed of the loose stones which filled it up, leading to the apprehension that, if this stone be not made secure, the entire chamber may shortly become a ruin.

On entering the chamber, which is about four feet square, and nearly five feet in height, above the upright stones forming its walls, are observed seven projecting flags forming a beehive roof capped by a large horizontal flag, elaborately covered with devices, several of which extend out of sight under the structure, and where no tool could reach ; again affording evidence that the sculptures upon this stone also must have been executed before the erection of the carn.

In removing the loose stones which had fallen into this chamber, on the centre of the floor was found a circle of earth, about a foot in diameter, enclosing about a hatful of charred bones, which were covered with a flag. Over the flag were raised, for about two feet in height, alternate layers of finely broken and larger stones, among which were found some human teeth, and twenty-four bones, each about four inches long, one of which, in the broken state in which it was found, is here represented full size. The double row of processes, or notched projections, on its lower extremity, will identify it as the smaller and lower of the two large bones in the leg of a kid : and the presence of so many of these particular bones here, whatever else they may have been intended to indicate, may point to the sacrifice of half a dozen of these animals.

No. 12.

On entering the chamber, the first stone on the left, here represented, measures four feet six inches in height, two feet nine inches in breadth, and is of an average thickness of ten inches. A stone, No. 13,

standing in the south-west angle of the chamber, measures three feet
ten inches in height, three feet in breadth, and eight inches in thickness; but has no devices sculptured upon it.

No. 14.

This stone, No. 14, which faces the entrance of the chamber, and
passage into the interior, is inscribed in a very remarkable manner.
It measures four feet three inches in height, three feet two inches
in width, and nine inches in average thickness.

No. 15.

The northern wall of the western chamber is formed by this stone,
measuring three feet seven inches in height, two feet ten inches in
breadth, and one foot in thickness.

No. 16, on the right-hand side of the entrance to the chamber, has
been already described.

The dimensions of the northern chamber are very similar to the other two before described. Since the removal of the loose stones which filled up the interior, the upright stones forming its walls have become much depressed by the superincumbent weight of loose stones above them ; and if not soon placed again erect, this chamber must inevitably become a ruin, a catastrophe which all students of archæology would have just reason to regret.

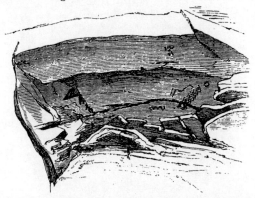

Lower surfaces of lintel and roofing stone over northern chamber.

The chamber has a beehive roof, formed by five flags projecting inwards, and covered in by a horizontal one, on which are *cut in very fine lines,* less than a quarter of an inch asunder, among other devices, four remarkable chevron lines, about one foot in length. The characters sculptured on the lower surface of the lintel and of the roofing stone are very carefully represented in the above woodcut.

No. 17.

The stone here represented forms the left-hand or western side of

F

the northern chamber, and measures four feet high, three feet wide, and one foot thick.   In the remote left-hand angle of the chamber, as in the western one, stands an upright, marked No. 18 on the plan, measuring three feet two inches in height, two feet wide, and seven inches thick.   Neither of these two angular uprights shows any evidence of being sculptured, and their use in the construction is not

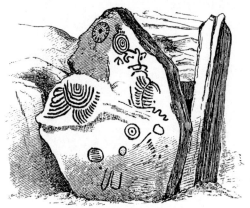

No. 20.

apparent.   No devices have been detected on the stone facing the entrance to this chamber, marked No. 19 on the plan, measuring three feet six inches high, four feet five inches wide, and nine inches thick.

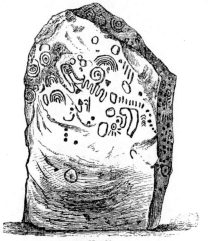

No. 21.

The stone, No. 20, constituting the eastern side of the northern chamber, measures four feet five inches in height, three feet four inches at its widest part, and is about five inches thick.   The stone, No. 31, across the lower part of the entrance to this chamber, is one foot ten inches in height, two feet two inches in width, and eight inches in thickness; and is devoid of any inscription.

Extending from the northern chamber to the termination of the passage stands a stone, No. 21, with very remarkable sculptures, not

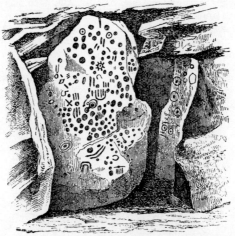

Nos. 22 and 23.

only on its face, but also upon the ledge abutting on the passage.   It measures five feet eight inches in height, three feet six inches in width, one foot in thickness, and is here very accurately represented.

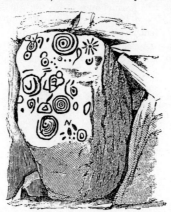

No. 24.

The two terminal stones on the north side of the passage, with the devices upon them, are shown together above, No. 22 measuring five feet seven inches in height, three feet nine inches in breadth, and ten inches in thickness; while No. 23 measures four feet in height, fourteen inches in breadth of face, and is fifteen inches in receding depth.

The devices on the second stone, No. 24, on the right-hand or north side of the passage, will be found delineated on the previous page. It stands three feet six inches high, two feet eight inches broad, and is nine inches thick.

On No. 25, the first stone on the right of the passage, measuring two feet six inches in height, two feet seven inches in width, and one foot in thickness, no devices, if any such ever existed, are now traceable.

The stone, No. 27, standing across the end of the passage where it

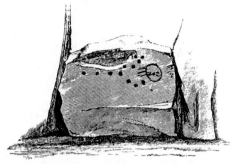

No. 27.

opens into the large central chamber, measures two feet five inches in width, and also in height, and seven inches in thickness, having its eastern face marked as here shown. No 28, also standing across the passage, between Nos. 4 and 5 on the south, and No. 23 on the north side, measures two feet two inches in height, is two feet wide, and one foot thick; but is quite devoid of sculptures of any kind.

We found a loose fragment of an inscribed rock, here represented,

Fragment of inscribed rock.

standing two feet eight inches in height, near the entrance to the passage; but it would be impossible to decide to what portion of the carn it originally belonged. We left it standing on the north side of the entrance, near the place where it was found.

It would be an irreparable loss to archæology if this historic pile were now allowed to become a wreck, for want of a little timely and inexpensive repair. The only thing necessary to be done would be to remove temporarily the loose stones over the northern and western chambers; and, after carefully and skilfully resetting the uprights and broken lintel, to replace the loose stones in their original position, as their weight could only serve to give firmness to the structure, should the parietal stones be properly poised.

It is to be hoped that the various articles found during our explorations of the carns at Loughcrew, in 1865, will be soon arranged and classified, so that antiquaries may be able to examine and refer to them, as might be required.

They were presented by us to the National Museum of the Royal Irish Academy, on the part of the late lord of the soil, J. L. W. Naper, Esq., who consented to part with them, for the Nation's sake, with an amount of public patriotism and high minded generosity which reflected credit upon his large and liberal heart.

APPENDIX.

ON 4th April, 1857, Rev. James H. Todd, D. D., President of the Royal Irish Academy, applied by letter addressed to His Excellency the Lord Lieutenant to have the manuscript materials collected for the illustration of local history and antiquities during the progress of the Ordnance Survey, transferred from the Office of the Survey in the Phœnix Park to the Library of the Royal Irish Academy. After some delay arising from the necessity which existed for arranging, indexing, and otherwise preparing the volumes for binding, at length, on 30th November, 1860, 103 volumes of MS. papers, containing information relating to the local history and antiquities of Ireland, together with eleven volumes of sketches of various objects of antiquarian interest, were duly presented, in accordance with the authority of the Right Honorable the Secretary of State for War, to the Royal Irish Academy. From the volume relating to Meath we quote the following letter of Dr. O'Donovan on the parish of Loughcrew, as it will show exactly how little was then known of the real history of this very remarkable place :—

"KELLS, 30*th July*, 1836.

"Near the church there is a holy well which retains the name of the great *Saint Kieran*, and should be called Tober Kieran on the Ordnance Map. The parish has derived its name from a lake called Loch Cροιбе, i. e. the lake of the bush or tree. It contains one island planted with beautiful large sallow or willow trees, but the lake has not derived its name from these. Every place in Ireland bearing the name of *creeve* had originally a *sacred tree of widely extending branches*, planted for the purpose of inauguration, or to commemorate the death of some famous personage. Lough*creeve* would be the most analogical spelling of this name; but custom has too well established Lough*crew* for us to attempt a change of it.

"There are three hills about a mile asunder in this parish, having three heaps [carns] of stones on their summits, with which the following wild legend is connected. A famous old hag of antiquity, called Cailleach Bhéartha (Calliagh Vērǎ), came one time from the north to perform a magical feat in this neighbourhood, by which she was to obtain great power, if she succeeded. She took an apron full of stones, and dropped a *carn* on *Carnbane;* from this she jumped to the summit of Slieve Na Cally, a mile distant, and dropped a second carn there: from this hill she made a second jump, and dropped a carn on another hill, about a mile distant. If she could make another leap, and drop the fourth carn, it appears that the magical feat would be accomplished; but in giving the jump, she slipped and fell in the townland of Patrickstown, in the parish of Diamor, where she broke her neck. Here she was buried; and her grave was to be seen not many years ago in the field called Cúl a' móta (i. e. back of the moat), about two hundred perches to the east of the moat in that townland ; but it is now destroyed.

" This is the very old lady whose shade still haunts the *lake* and carn of Slieve Guillion in the county of Armagh. Her name was *Evlin*, and it would appear from some legends about her that she was of De Danannite origin.

" She is now a Banshee in some parts of Ireland, and is represented in some elegies as appearing before the deaths of some persons. I know nothing more about her, but that on one occasion she turned the celebrated Fin Mac Cooil into a grey old man ; but his soldiers dug through the mountain of Slieve Guillion in Armagh until they drove her out of her cave, and forced her to restore Fin to his former beauty and symmetry.

" Does her name, Eıblín bheupťa ınġın Ġhuılınn, appear in the genealogies of the Tuatha De Dananns?

" A quatrain of her poetic composition is yet repeated at Carnbane, but I calculate it is a post-original :—

> Mıre Cailleaó bhéupťa ḃoćṫ
> lomḃa ıcnġnaḃ ḃ' aṁaṗcaṗ ṗıaṁ
> Chonaıceaṗ Cápn bán 'na loć
> Ġıḃ ġo ḃṗuıl anoıṗ 'na ṗlıaḃ.

I am poor Cailleach Bera,
Many a wonder I have ever seen—
I have seen Carnbane a lake,
Though now a mountain green.

What a pity that she is not alive now to throw light upon geology ! Could Mr. Curry, from his vast knowledge of fairyology and *hagi*ology, give me any account of the old *hag* who left her name on this range and on Slieve Guillion?

" There is an eminence in the townland of Knocklough called Slieve Guillion, and a rude *stone chair* on the summit of Slieve Nacally called caťaoıṗ na caıllıġe beupťa, i. e. *Calliagh Bera's Chair*. It is a large stone, about two tons weight, ornamented with a cross sunk (cut) into the seat of the chair, in which three might sit together. This hollow seems to have been made in the stone with a hammer : the cross is probably the work of a modern stonecutter. The back of the chair was broken by some human enemy to old Evlin."

As it may serve to render the map at page 22 more intelligible, and probably also prove interesting and useful to the general reader, or antiquary who may visit the place, which is most accessible by railway route to Oldcastle, we here subjoin a succinct account of the remains of the other carns indicated on the map by the letters of the alphabet.

Commencing at the western extremity of the range, on the hill popularly known as Carnbawn, which attains a height of 842 feet above the sea level, we come to

A.

Nearly all the stones which formed this carn have been removed. Its present remains are seven yards in diameter, and are situated sixty-six yards south-east of D. Four large stones still remain, marking out the circumference of its base.

A².

In a plantation, at a distance of 130 yards south of D, the remains of a carn are visible, but nearly level with the ground. It is nine yards in diameter. One large stone still stands upright on the circumference.

A³.

On the southern scalp of the hill, in a most conspicuous position, sixty yards south-west from D, and nearly close to the southern side of the present deer-park wall, once stood a carn twenty-two yards in diameter. Its present remains are not more than a foot or two in height, consisting chiefly of small fragmentary stones, the *debris* of the former carn, and these are now covered with green grass.

B.

Forty-six yards to the west of D are the remains of a carn seven yards in diameter. The loose stones which formed it are nearly all gone, leaving in the centre three large flags, laid on edge, forming a chamber twelve feet in length, and two feet in breadth, pointing in the direction of E 20° S. In clearing out this chamber several fragments of charred bones, which had acquired an unusual degree of heaviness, were found mixed with the earth at the bottom.

C.

Sixty yards to the south-west of D will be found the remains of a carn, five yards in diameter. Nearly all the stones have been removed, leaving only four large stones still marking the site. At the distance of twenty-five feet to the north of the carn now lies prostrate a pillar stone, which, like the celebrated Menhir* of Quintin (Côtes du Nord) which is nine metres over ground, formerly stood upon its smaller end. It measures seven feet long, three feet six inches broad, and one foot thick.

D.

This has been the largest of all the carns in the range, the diameter of its base being sixty yards. The north and east sides have been left untouched; but on the south and west for nearly 100 yards round the base, and extending inwards to a distance of twenty-four yards from the circumference towards the centre, the dry loose stones composing the carn have been entirely removed. The height of what remained of the carn, before commencing any operations upon it, measured twenty-eight paces in sloping ascent from the base to the summit. The original circle of fifty-four large flag stones, laid on edge round its base, is still perfect; and on the eastern side these marginal stones curve inwards for twelve paces in length towards a point indicated by E. 20° S., denoting where the entrance or passage to the interior chambers is to be found. As the carn at this point—which, judging from the analogy in the construction of the other carns, would indicate the direction of the passage or entrance—appeared not to have been previously disturbed, Mr. Naper and Mr. Hamilton had from the first strong hopes of finding the interior chambers and their contents in their original state, such exactly as they had been left in by the builders of this megalithic pile. Accordingly, on Monday morning, 4th September, 1865, about a dozen labouring men commenced to remove the stones, and to make a passage inwards from this point. As they advanced in this way into the carn, the loose stones composing it occasionally fell in dangerous masses, filling up excavations already made; so that it was at length determined to make a cutting right through the carn, running east and west, and commencing on the top. After two weeks spent in this labour,

---

* "Memoire sur les Monumens Primitifs," p. 17, par A. Carro: Paris, 1863.

and with as many men as could be conveniently engaged at it, we did not come upon any of the interior chambers ; nor have our labours been more success- ful on 3, 4, 5, 6, 8, 9, and 10, June, 1868, when, by Mr. Naper's direc- tions, twenty men were busily engaged every day in continuing the transverse cutting through the carn, in search of the interior chambers. This, however, is now the only one of all the carns left unexamined ; and, as the surface level of the ground has been already reached for the greater part of the way across the carn, very little additional labour would be required to settle the question whether or not this is a " blind tope."

As the cutting proceeded, about midway down among the loose stones, were found portions of skulls, teeth, and other bones of graminivorous animals, probably the ox and deer.

At a distance of 105 feet to the north-west of this carn, and on the very point of the escarpment of the hill, stood a pillar of quartz, eight feet high, three feet broad, and two feet thick. How far it may have entered the ground when being placed there originally, we have not ascertained. At present it is broken across a little above the ground, probably by lightning, and the upper portion now lies as it fell. At a very slight cost it could be raised to its ori- ginal erect position, which we would very much desire to see.

E.

Traces of this carn only sufficient to indicate the site remain ; and these show it to have been about five yards in diameter.

F.

About five feet in height of the original carn still remain. Its diameter is sixteen and a half yards. Clearing away the loose stones and earth which filled the centre showed the arrangement of the interior chambers to be in the form of a cross, the shaft, denoting the passage to the chambers represented by the top and arms of the cross, having a bearing of E. 10° N. The length of the passage is eight feet, and it is two feet two inches broad. The entire length from the commencement of the passage to the extremity of the opposite chamber is fifteen feet, and the breadth from the extremity of the southern to the extremity of the northern chamber is nine feet four inches. The com- mencement of the passage is not closed up by a block of stone, but merely by small loose stones laid against it. Only one of the roofing flags, covering the commencement of the passage, remains in its original position. Across the entrances of the southern and western chambers are laid stones, about a foot in height, and from four to five inches in thickness. On the floor of the northern crypt rests a rude sepulchral stone basin, three feet five inches long, two feet four inches broad, and five inches thick. Under this basin were found a portion of a bone pin and a flake of flint. In the south- western corner of the southern chamber, and about a foot from the bottom, was found, imbedded among the clay and stones which filled it up, a brown ironstone ball, three inches in diameter, and well rounded. Several frag- ments of bones lay scattered indiscriminately here and there upon the floor.

Eight of the stones in these chambers are sculptured, and on the south side, three of the original boundary stones enclosing the carn are still standing.

G.

G is twenty-one yards in diameter ; and is only one yard from F, and thirty-four and a half yards from D. Eight large stones stand in the margin. Traces only sufficient to indicate the site of the carn remain, all the interior chamber stones having disappeared.

H.

The present remains of this carn are between five and six feet in height, and eighteen yards in diameter; it is sixteen and a half yards from L, the second largest carn on the western hill. Some curious attempts at dry masonry will be found at the northern and southern extremities of the chambers. The covering of the interior chambers had entirely disappeared, with the exception of about half a dozen large overlapping flags, giving a good example of the mode of roofing, which are still to be seen in their places over the western and northern crypts; and what remained of the loose stones forming the carn had become entirely overgrown with grass, exposing its contents to the destructive influences of rain and frost. After carefully clearing out the central chambers, the plan was found to be cruciform, nearly similar to F, except that the central chamber might be considered a rude octagon. The passage, which has a bearing of E. 10° S., is thirteen feet long, two feet wide at the commencement, and four feet wide at the extremity. The entire length from the beginning of the passage to the extremity of the opposite or western chamber is twenty-four feet; and the distance across the other two chambers is sixteen feet. The breadth of the southern chamber is two feet seven inches; of the western chamber four feet at rear, diminishing towards its entrance to three feet two inches; of the northern chamber, four feet two inches, on the floor of which rests a rude stone basin, four feet three inches long, four feet broad, and about six inches thick. Loose stones and earth filled the unroofed chambers and passage on the top of the carn for about a foot and a half in depth. The passage itself, from that to the bottom, a depth of about three feet, was completely packed with bones in a fragmentary state, nearly all showing evidences of having been burnt, and were found mixed with several small fragments of quartz.

The three chambers were found filled with an indiscriminate mixture of stones, broken bones, and earth; the latter in a soft, stiff, retentive state, although the weather had been previously very fine. This mixture was picked and removed with great care; and in it were obtained, apparently without having been placed there in any definite order, one end of a bone bodkin; one half of a bone ferrule; six pieces of bone pins;* one tine of an antler, three inches long; fourteen fragments of very rude brown earthenware or pottery, evidently portions of urns, much blackened by fire, particularly on the inside surface; ten pieces of flint; upwards of 200 sea shells, principally limpet and cockle shells, in a tolerably perfect state of preservation, and 110 other shells in a broken state; eight varieties of small lustrous or shining stones; upwards of 100 white sea pebbles†, and about sixty others of different shades of colour, and all of various sizes.

At the back of the western chamber was found a small brown stone ball,

---

* One ornamented bone pin, an inch and three-quarters in length, still retains the metallic rivet which fastened on a head.

† D^r. Pennant, F. R. S., who published an account of his Western Tour in Scotland in 1771, has described most of the carns as formed of round stones from the shore. This may have arisen from the supposition that such stones possessed peculiar virtues or holiness, because he mentions some round black ones, preserved in the Cathedral of Oransay, upon which the people made oaths that were regarded as more binding than any others. In the "Letters from the Irish Highlands" it is said to be customary for mothers to pile

and just inside its entrance, about two-thirds* of a circular flat bone disc, about six inches in diameter, being the greater portion of one of the intercostal bones inserted between the vertebræ in the skeleton of a whale.

Underneath the stone basin in the northern chamber were found imbedded in damp earth, and mixed with small splinters of burnt bones, six balls, the largest about an inch in diameter, but in so soft a state, that they could scarcely be touched without injuring them. Five of these are white carbonate of lime, and the sixth is a dark-coloured ball of the same material, but made from some rock of a coralline structure. An account of the probable origin and use of these balls will be found in the description of carn L, in which eight similar ones were discovered. In the southern chamber, and about the entrance to it, while carefully picking and removing a very miscellaneous collection of stones, broken bones, and stiff retentive earth with which it had become filled up, we obtained articles of glass, amber, bronze, and even iron ; together with the remains of a large number of bone implements, the names and uses of which have not yet been satisfactorily determined.

Of glass, we collected three small beads, of different shapes, one green, and two blue; two fragments, or splinters of glass ; a tapering trumpet-shaped piece of hollow glass, one inch in length, and resembling in appearance a shark's tooth or a Rupert's drop.

Of amber, we found seven small beads, the largest scarcely a quarter of an inch in diameter, and another small oblong bead of uncertain material.

Of bronze, we obtained six open rings (that is, not closed into one solid piece), varying from a quarter to three quarters of an inch in diameter ; a portion of another which is hollow and formed by the overlapping of a thin plate of bronze ; and portions of eight other small rings, in a less perfect state of preservation.

In some few instances where the bone implements chanced to be protected by an overlying stone, their original polish is still perfect ; in all other cases they were found in a state as soft as cheese, and could with difficulty be ex-

---

round white stones on the graves of their children; and a similar practice is described by some of our travellers as prevailing along the eastern coast of Africa.

Lieutenant-Colonel Forbes Leslie in his "Early Races of Scotland," Vol. II., p. 319, on the authority of Martin's *Western Isles*, tells us that—"in Scotland 'the black stones of Iona' were so called, although of a grey colour, from the dread penalties which were supposed to attach to any one who swore falsely upon them. It was on them that the Kings of the Isles, on bended knees, and with uplifted hands, swore to preserve inviolate the rights of their vassals. In another of the Western Isles, Martin describes a stone of a green colour, about the size of a goose's egg, on which, in cases of importance, the people were accustomed to take oaths. This stone was called '*Baul Mulay*,' and was then (in the end of the 17th century) preserved with great care by its hereditary guardian. The same author mentions an altar and a blue stone in Fladda, an islet near the coast of Skye. On this stone the people were wont to swear in cases of peculiar interest ; but it had other mystical properties besides the infliction of penalties on those who violated their oaths, for persons desirous of procuring a fair wind poured water over this stone before proceeding on their voyage. The 'Stone of Odin,' a portion of the celebrated monument of Stennis in Orkney, witnessed vows that were deemed peculiarly sacred. In the same island, in 1438, mention is made of individuals sworn on the Hirdman-Stein. The stone of Plougoumelen, in the Pays de Vannes in Brittany, still insures the sanctity of an oath."

* The remaining portion of this disc was found on 9th June, 1868, in picking the debris thrown out of the carn.

tracted from the stiff earth without breaking them. Such, indeed, was their soft state, that we believe they could not have been preserved for many years longer, and probably many have become entirely decomposed. The shapes of several will be found peculiar and different, and well worth the careful study of the antiquary. Many of them resemble in size and shape the flint knives of Scandinavia, one of which, from the collection in the Royal Irish Academy, is here engraved the actual size.

Scandinavian Flint Knife: actual size.

We have been enabled to save 4071 fragments of these in a plain state—once polished, but without further ornamentation: 108, nearly perfect in shape; 60, where the bone material is little decomposed, and still retains the original polish ; 27 fragments which appear to have been stained ; 12 plain fragments perforated by a single hole near the end; 500 fragments ornamented with rows of fine parallel transverse lines, and two others similarly ornamented, and perforated near the end ; 13 combs, 7 of which are engraved on both sides, the heads only and the roots of the teeth of the combs now remaining : 91 implements engraved by compass, and in a very high order of art, with circles, curves, ornamental puncturings, &c., and twelve of these decorated on both sides. In some instances the perforations near the end appear to have been counter-sunk. In all there are 4884 pieces.

In the whole collection there is but a single instance of any attempt to delineate any living thing. The following, made up of two fragments joined together, we take to be intended for the representation of an antlered stag ; and we have made very diligent, but unsuccessful search among the inscribed fragments for as much as would complete the outline of the animal.

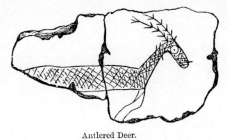

Antlered Deer.

Soon after the discovery of these inscribed bone flakes we placed them in the hands of the present Bishop of Limerick, the Right Rev. Charles Graves, D. D., then President of the Royal Irish Academy, who undertook to describe their peculiar ornamentation in the "Transactions of the Academy." Regret-

ting that the promised description has not yet appeared, and in the hope of soon
seeing a learned disquisition on the age, character, and style of the ornaments
employed, we simply here submit the following *fac simile* engravings of a

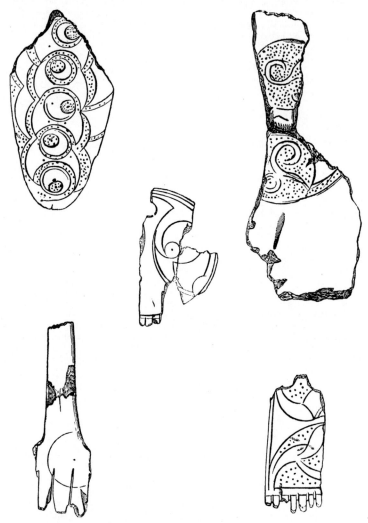

Specimens of inscribed Bone Implements.

few of them, wishing at the same time to record our obligations and our
thanks to **Dr.** Graves for having in the meantime permitted us to take electro-
type copies, here used, from his wood-blocks.

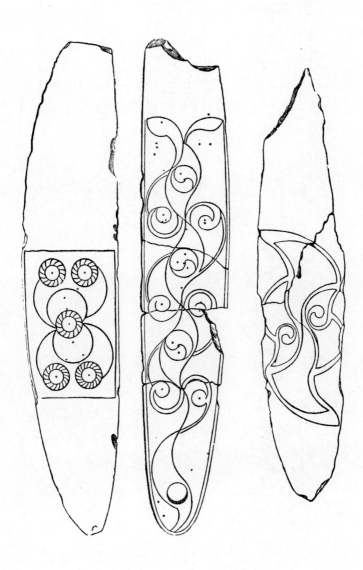

Specimens of inscribed Bone Implements.

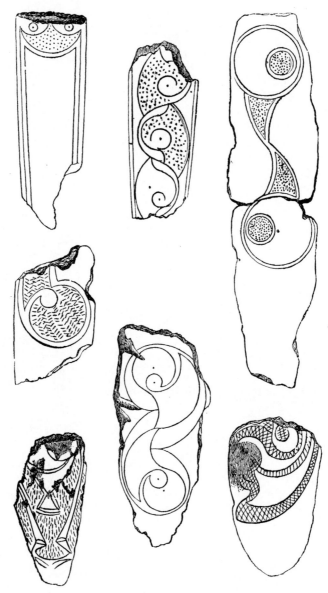

Specimens of inscribed Bone Implements.

Not lying together, but mixed up with the earth and *debris* which filled the southern chamber, we found in all seven specimens of iron objects, all thickly incrusted with rust. One is an open ring, about half an inch in diameter; one half of another, somewhat larger; two pieces, each about an inch long, and a quarter of an inch thick, of uncertain use ; and one thin piece, three quarters of an inch long, and half an inch broad. The two remaining pieces are here engraved the actual size, the rust having been removed from their respective points; the smaller one, we submit, presenting all the appearance of having been one leg of a pair of compasses, an instrument with which the bone implements were evidently inscribed and ornamented; and the larger piece is unmistakeably an iron punch or pick, with a flat point or working end, the head or larger end bearing incontestable evidence of the use of the hammer. Many of the figures, particularly the circular ones, found inscribed upon the stones in these carns, have been executed in *punched* or picked work, in several instances each impact or stroke in the line being still quite visible ; and it is possible that such a tool as this may have been used in their execution.

From the passage and crypts of this carn we collected, and have preserved for anatomical examination a large trunkful of human bones, many in a charred state, and apparently having belonged to individuals of various ages and sexes.

All the foregoing articles were found during our first examination of this ruined carn in September, 1865 ; and on Tuesday evening, 9th June, 1868, we commenced to pick over slowly and carefully the *debris* which, after a previous careful picking, had been thrown out from the bottom of the carn in which this highly interesting collection of antiquarian objects had been obtained in 1865. Assisted by two men, we continued the picking the following day, and our labour was rewarded by finding some perfect, and several hundred fragments of, polished bone implements, five of them being beautifully ornamented; a dozen of small open bronze rings of different sizes, several limpet and cockle shells, and white sea-pebbles; half of an iron ring, and a piece of iron attached by rust to a broken off end of one of the bone implements; a small stone ball, about the size of a boy's ordinary marble, having a white vein, such as is seen in agate, running across it ; a thin rectangular piece of smoothed stone, about an inch long, and consisting of alternate layers of pink and bluish grey shades of colour; two bone beads ; a green and also a blue glass bead ; an object

Iron Tools.

in glass, such as in the Catalogue of the R. I. A., p. 163, fig. 118, is called a " double bead," half an inch in length, without any hole passing through it, somewhat in the shape of an hour-glass, without being so attenuated in the middle, and displaying an exquisitely soft shade of green colour when held up to the light; a ring about half an inch in diameter and nearly worn across

H

at one place, apparently of that species of talc known as steatite or soap stone; a flint nodule, about the size of a boy's marble, of sponge shape, the part originally adhering to the rock remaining in its natural condition, while all the rest of the surface was smoothly polished, exhibiting shades of brown and white, and making on the whole a very pretty ornament; and a portion of an intercostal bone from the skeleton of a whale. All these were left at Loughcrew House.

In this carn there are seven inscribed stones.

I.

This carn is 64½ yards to the east of F, 53 yards S. W. of L, and is 21 yards in diameter. The apex of the carn itself has disappeared, leaving from four to five feet only in height of the original structure, wanting the slabs by which the interior chambers had been covered. These crypts had become filled up with small stones, by the removal of the roof. Directly over the chambers a thick crop of luxuriant nettles flourished, and struck their roots down into the interstices of some of the laminated flagstones forming the chambers. During the progress of clearing out the interior, we had thus the mortification of seeing portions of some of the engraved stones crumble down, forced out by these nettle roots, before we were able to make any record of the devices on them. The direction of the entrance is due east. The passage alone is eight feet six inches long, and four feet six inches wide; and the distance from the commencement of the passage to the back of the opposite chamber is twenty-two feet; the diameter across the chambers north and south measures thirteen feet. The interior arrangement consists of seven compartments, formed by flagstones standing out towards the centre of the structure. The breadth of the first chamber on the left-hand side, which faces the north, is two feet eight inches; of the second, three feet six inches; of the third, shaped somewhat in the form of a triangle, three feet seven inches at the back, its widest part; of the fourth, three feet eight inches; of the fifth, three feet seven inches at the rear, and like the third chamber, narrowing considerably towards the entrance; of the sixth, three feet ten inches; and of the seventh, or last chamber, two feet eight inches.

On each of the floors of the first, second, fourth, and fifth chambers rested a square flag, about two square feet in area, and two inches thick. A quantity of charred bones was found on each of these flags: but in such a crushed state from the falling in of the stones upon them, that it would be difficult to determine to what portion of the frame they belonged. On lifting up the flag on which the bones had been placed, in each of these four compartments we found immediately underneath a layer, about four inches in depth, of dry small stones, the surface portion of the layer broken very fine, from a quarter of an inch to an inch in size, and having some fragments of charred bones scattered on top, the lower portion of the layer consisting of larger stones.

In the compartment which exactly faces the east, and on the surface of these finely broken stones we found two stone ornaments—a bead and a pendant. The bead lay about the centre of the space, covered by the flag; and the pendant under, but close to the extremity of the flag, on the right hand side, and near the back of the compartment. The bead has been highly polished, and its being narrower on one side than the other will show that it was worn in a circular form. We conjecture that both are portions of a necklace such as has been found in 1853 by M. L. Galles in the tumulus of

Tumiac, in Morbihan.* The greatest diameter of the bead is three-quarters of an inch; and the pendant, perforated by a single hole for suspension, is one inch and a quarter long. Both appear to have suffered from the action of fire; and have become so decomposed, that it is somewhat hazardous to name the materials of which they are formed. The bead, however, *resembles* pale gray earthy grit, which has become soft from the decomposition of the felspathic part of the stone, or more probably is blue carboniferous limestone; and the pendant *yellow shale* mixed with whitish particles.

The floor of the sixth compartment was covered with a closely fitting flag, three feet ten inches long, three feet three inches broad, and nine inches thick. We found no bones resting on its surface, as we had done on the other floor flags in the other compartments furnished with a slab; but on raising it we observed that it covered a layer of finely broken stones, mixed with splinters of charred bones, and having a depression of nearly a couple of inches in the centre. This stone, as it rested on the floor, concealed the sculpturing on the lower portion of the projecting slab to the west of it to a height of twenty-two inches from its base.

Eleven of the stones in this carn are inscribed.

J.

This carn is twenty-three yards N. E. of H, and only three yards distant from L. It is fifteen and a half yards in diameter, and its present remains from four to five feet in height, with twelve large stones still in the circumference. The interior had been much disturbed, but left filled up with loose stones and rubbish. The passage, having a bearing of E. 10° S., is seven feet six inches in length, without any upright stone closing its entrance. A roughly-finished brown stone ball, about an inch in diameter, was found near the opening of the passage into the interior chambers.

Three of the stones in this carn are inscribed.

K.

K is twelve and a half yards N. E. from L, and is sixteen and a half yards in diameter. When the interior was cleared out, the large flagstones forming the central chambers were found in a rather disorderly condition. The bearing of the entrance is E. 15° N. Thirteen stones remain round the margin, and no object of antiquarian interest was found here. At a distance of twenty feet to the south-east now lies a pillar stone, six feet long, two feet broad, and one foot thick.

Two of the chamber stones are inscribed.

L.

L is forty-five yards in diameter, surrounded by 42 large stones, laid lengthwise on their edges, and varying from six to twelve feet in length, and from four to five feet high. Great quantities of the loose stones which formed the apex of this carn have been removed, of which there are very visible evidences. A curve inwards in the circumference of ten yards in length, on each side of a point having a bearing of E. 20° S., indicates the direction of the entrance or passage which commences at a distance of eighteen feet inward from the circumference.

---

* "Description des objects de l'age de la pierre polie :" Vannes: Imprimerie de L. Galles, 1867.

Finding a large flag on the top of the mutilated carn, we removed it and two others before we observed that we were actually taking to pieces what remained of the original construction of the roof. The principal portion of the overlapping flags which formed the roof over the chambers had disappeared, leaving them filled up with the loose stones which had fallen in. When the chambers were carefully cleared of these small stones, they exhibited *in situ* about forty of the large plinths which formed the matchless, dry, cyclopean masonry of the roof. This dome was constructed of large slabs overlapping one another, and bevelled slightly upwards, having most ingeniously inserted between them thinner slabs, which, on receiving the superincumbent weight, became crushed, and formed a bond for the whole. Wherever this precaution of placing thinner slabs or smaller stones between the larger ones was omitted, the larger slabs themselves are now found cracked across. What at present remains of this unique roofing rises twelve feet above the level of the floor, which is even with the ordinary surface of the ground. The breadth of the passage at the commencement is one foot ten inches, which increases to upwards of three feet about the middle, and contracts again to one foot nine inches where it terminates. The passage itself is twelve feet long; and the entire length, from the commencement of the passage to the extremity of the western chamber, is twenty-nine feet. The greatest breadth across the chambers is thirteen feet two inches, measured from nearly north and south points, diminishing to ten feet four inches where the passage terminates.

The seven chambers composing the interior of this great tomb are quadrangular and nearly square; the first on the left-hand side, at the termination of the passage, is four feet eight inches in breadth; the second three feet six inches; the third two feet two inches; the fourth four feet three inches; the fifth five feet ten inches; the sixth three feet five inches; and the seventh two feet six inches.

From among the loose stones which filled up the chamber we collected 1010 portions of bones; two bone flakes similar to those found in carn H; 154 fragments of very rude pottery, varying in size from one to thirty square inches. Some fragments retain their original brown colour, but the generality of them are much blackened by fire on the inside surface, and for a distance round the exterior of the lip, or upper rim of the urns, of which they were parts. One piece, a portion of the upper edge of an urn, about three inches long and three broad, is very rudely ornamented with three slight ridges; and about an inch from the top is perforated by a single hole. Another larger piece, ornamented with four slightly raised ridges, is perforated by two holes, one an inch and a half below the other.

Mr. Bateman[*] mentions urns with similar perforations, which he supposes were for suspension, and which he classes as incense urns. On this subject Canon Greenwell writes to us on 28th March, 1868:—

"The so-called incense cups have generally holes in the sides, sometimes near the top, at other times near the bottom. Most frequently they have two holes, but these increase in number until I have seen as many as twenty-seven, and I know of three or four 'incense cups' with open-work sides, which is only an extension of the holes. These 'incense cups' are small, like ordinary pot salt-cellars, while the fragments you found are of larger vessels. I have a cinerary urn sixteen inches high, which has two holes, and I have fragments of domestic vessels of large size pierced. The large urn

---

[*] "Ten Years' Diggings in Celtic and Saxon Grave Hills," by Thomas Bateman, p. 282. London: J. R. Smith, 36, Soho-square; Derby: W. Bemrose and Sons.

(sixteen inches) could never be suspended by means of the holes, nor can it be for suspension that incense cups have twenty-seven holes. Some other use must be found
for them."

We believe the specimens now found are new in this country—at least
we have not seen, nor have we heard of any such having been found in Ireland before this date.

Extending along the floor of the passage, completely covering it, and in-
clining a little way into the space surrounded by the interior chambers, seven
in number, lies a flag eight feet nine inches long, three feet six inches broad,
and about six inches thick. Close around the western end of this stone the earth
on the floor, to a depth of about two inches, was perfectly black, arising,
it appeared to us, from the presence of blackened ashes; from which it may
probably be inferred that the process of cremation was performed on this
stone.

On the floor of the second chamber, and shut in by an upright stone of
a foot high and four inches thick, rests a quadrangular stone basin, hollowed
out from the sides towards the centre, to a depth of three and a quarter inches,
and having a piece taken out of one of its sides. It measures two feet eleven
inches in length by two feet broad, and is about six inches in thickness.
Mixed with the earth under this sepulchral basin were found many fragments
of charred bones and several human teeth. Above we present a view of the
fifth or opposite chamber.

The broader end of the oval-shaped stone dish or basin points to the east, the narrower to the west. Its greatest length is five feet nine inches; at a distance of eighteen inches from the narrower extremity it is three feet one inch broad, and at eighteen inches from the other extremity it is seven inches broader, where, on the side facing the chambers, a curve of about four inches broad has been scooped out of the side of the stone. A raised rim, running all round it, varies from two to four inches in breadth, rising about an inch above the otherwise perfectly level surface of the stone, which has been tooled or picked.

After the interior chambers had been cleared of all the loose stones, &c., which had filled them up, on Tuesday evening, 19th September, 1865, in presence of Mr. Naper, Mr. Hamilton, Archbishop Errington, and a number of ladies, we turned up this remarkable stone basin, and beneath it were revealed to view several splinters of charred and blackened bones, with about a dozen small pieces of charcoal lying in various directions. On carefully picking the damp stiff earth underneath it, we found imbedded in it upwards of 900 pieces of charred bones; forty-eight human teeth in a very perfect state of preservation; the pointed end of a bone pin, five and a quarter inches long, and a quarter of an inch thick; a fragment, about an inch in length, of a similar bone pin; a most perfectly rounded syenite ball, still preserving its original polish—nearly two and three-quarter inches in diameter; another perfectly round stone ball, streaked with white and purple layers, and about an inch in diameter; another stone ball, upwards of three-quarters of an inch in diameter, of a brown colour, dashed with dark spots; a finely-polished jet-like object, oval in shape, an inch and a quarter in length, and three-quarters of an inch broad; eight white balls (carbonate of lime), which had become quite soft; but which gradually dried, on exposure, to a sufficient degree of hardness to enable us to take them away in a tolerable state of preservation.

These latter, as well as the five similar ones found in carn H (see p. 52), we consider were "brain balls," won and worn as trophies during life by the champion laid here to his rest, and finally, after death, deposited with his ashes. We here present engravings of two of them (*b* and *c*) in their present actual size.

a   *b*   *c*

The ball (*a*) has been previously referred to at page 52, and is here given simply to show the coralline character of its structure. Of the soft white balls the best preserved specimen (*b*) is here accurately represented; and most of the others have become rubbed down very much to the size and appearance of (*c*).

In confirmation of the custom of making these "brain balls," we quote the following extract from one of Professor O'Curry's Lectures " On the Manuscript Materials of Ancient Irish History," p. 275. The account is taken from a tale of great historical interest, namely, the tale of the tragic end of Conchobor M'Nessa, King of Ulster, who died of the effects of a wound inflicted on him by a *ball* made of the brains of the champion *Mesgedhra*, King of Leinster, the story being preserved in the " Book of Leinster" and other vellum MSS. of great authority :—

" One of those barbarous military customs which, in one form or another, prevailed in former times perhaps all over the world, and which have been preserved in some countries nearly down to our own days, existed in Erinn at this period.

" Whenever one champion slew another in single combat, it is stated that he cut off his head, if possible, clove it open, took out the brain, and mixing this with lime, rolled it up into a ball, which he then dried, and placed in the armoury of his territory or province, among the trophies of his nation.

" As an instance of this strange custom, we have already seen, in the sketch of *Aithirné*,* the poet (in speaking of the siege of *Beann Edair*,† or Howth), that, on that occasion, when the great Ulster champion, *Conall Cearnach*,‡ pursued *Mesgedhra*,§ the King of Leinster, from Howth to Claena|| (in the present county of Kildare), where he overtook and fought him in single combat, he cut off the king's head after he had killed him, and extracted the brain. And, according to that story, it appears that after having put it through the usual process for hardening and preservation, he placed the ball formed of the royal brain among the precious trophies of Ulster, in the great house of the Royal Branch at Emania, where it continued to be esteemed as an object of great provincial interest and pride.

" Now, Conor Mac Nessa, in accordance with the custom of the times, had two favourite fools at his court ; and these silly, though often cunning, persons having observed the great respect in which *Mesgedhra's* brain was held by their betters, and wishing to enjoy its temporary possession, stole it out of the armoury and took it out to the lawn of the court, where they began to play with it as a common ball.

" While thus one day thoughtlessly engaged, *Cet Mac Magach*,¶ a famous Connacht champion, whose nation was at war with Conor Mac Nessa, happened to come up to them in disguise; and perceiving, and soon recognising, the precious ball which they were carelessly throwing from hand to hand, he had little difficulty in obtaining it from them. Having thus unexpectedly secured a prize of honour so valuable, *Cet* returned immediately into Connacht; and as there was a prophecy that *Mesgedhra* would avenge himself upon the Ulstermen, he never went forth upon any border excursion or adventure without carrying the king's brain with him in his girdle, hoping by it to fulfil the prophecy by the destruction of some important chief or champion among the Ulster warriors.

" Shortly after this time *Cet*, at the head of a strong party of the men of Connacht, carried off a large prey and plunder from Southern Ulster ; but they were pursued and overtaken (at *Bailé-ath-an-Urchair*,** now Ardnurchar, in the present county of Westmeath) by the Ulstermen, under the command of the king himself. Both sides halted on the banks of a stream, which they selected as an appropriate battle-field, and prepared for combat. *Cet* soon discovered that the pursuit was led by King Conor, at once bethought him of the prophecy ; and immediately laid his plan for its fulfilment. Accordingly, perceiving that a large number of the ladies of Connacht, who had come out to greet the return of their husbands, had placed themselves on a hill near the scene of the intended battle, he concealed himself among them.

" Now, at this time, when two warriors or two armies were about to engage in battle, it was the custom for the women, if any were present, of either party to call upon any distinguished chief or champion from the opposite side to approach them and exhibit himself to their view, that they might see if his beauty, dignity, and martial bearing were equal to what fame had reported them to be.

---

* Pronounced *Ahirne.*   † Pronounced *Benn Edar.*
‡ Pronounced *Konall Kerna.*   § Pronounced *Mesgedra.*
|| Pronounced *Kleena.*   ¶ Pronounced *Ket mac Maga.*
** Pronounced *Bally Ah-an-urkur.*

" To carry out his plan, then *Cet* instructed the Connacht women to invite Conor himself to come forward that they might view him. To this request Conor willingly assented, in the spirit of the chivalry of the time, but when he had come within a short distance of the presence of the ladies, on the corresponding eminence at his own side of the stream, *Cet* raised himself in their midst, and fixed Mesgedhra's brain in his *Cranntabhailt** or sling. Conor perceived the movement, and recognising at once a mortal enemy, retreated as fast as he could to his own people ; however, just as he was entering the little grove of *Doiréda Bhaeth*,† *Cet*, who followed him closely, cast from the sling the ball made from the fatal brain, and succeeded in striking Conor with it on the head, lodging the ball in his skull.

" Conor's chief physicians were immediately in attendance, and after a long examination and consultation, they reported that it was not expedient to remove the ball ; and the royal patient was carried home, where he was so well attended by them, that after some time he recovered his usual health and activity. He was, however, charged to be careful to avoid, among other things, all violent exercise, riding on horseback, and all excitement or anger.

" He continued thus for years to enjoy good health, until the very day of the Crucifixion, when, observing the eclipse of the sun, and the atmospheric terrors of that terrible day, he asked *Bacrach*,‡ his druid, what the cause of it was.

" The druid consulted his oracles, and answered by informing the king that Jesus Christ, the Son of the living God, was at that moment suffering at the hands of the Jews. ' What crime has he committed ?' said Conor. ' None,' said the druid. ' Then are they slaying him innocently ?' said Conor. ' They are,' said the druid. Then Conor burst into sudden fury at the words, drew his sword, and rushed out to the wood of *Lamhraidhé*,§ which was opposite his palace door, where he began to hew down the young trees there, exclaiming in a rage : ' Oh! if I were present, it is thus I would cut down the enemies of the innocent man !' His rage continued to increase, until at last the fatal ball which was lodged in his skull started from its place, followed by the king's brain, and Conor Mac Nessa fell dead on the spot. This occurrence happened in the fortieth year of his reign ; and he has been counted ever since as the first man who died for the sake of Christ in Ireland.

" This curious tale seems to have always been believed by the Irish historians, and from a very early date. In one version of it, however (that in the Book of Leinster), it is stated that probably it was not from his druid that Conor received the information concerning the crucifixion of our Lord, but from Altus, a Roman consul."

The chief part of the very remarkable sculpturings on the large upright stone in the rear of the basin have been executed in *punched* work, but the six triangular figures, which of necessity are here given a little in excess of their relative dimensions, in order to show how the lines impinge, have been regularly grooved or *cut* into the stone, but not so deeply sunk as the other figures.

On the lower surface of the second large roofing flag, above the upright, and directly over the great sepulchral basin, is a reticulated pattern, finely cut, nine inches long, and varying from three to four inches in breadth, formed by twelve short lines crossing in a slanting direction eight other nearly parallel lines, and so forming about forty quadrilateral figures, varying from half an inch to an inch in breadth, and from an inch to an inch and a half in length.

We should perhaps have previously observed that the large flagstones constituting the chambers in this as well as in the other carns are, as to material, of a uniform character, consisting of compact sandy grit, the natural rock of the locality. The upright stone, however, on the western side of the basin in

---

* Pronounced *Krann Tabull.*　　　　† Pronounced *Derry da Bay.*
‡ Pronounced *Bacra.*　　　　§ Pronounced *Lam Roye.*

this carn is an exception, being a good specimen of a water-washed column of blue limestone, probably from some of the adjoining lakes ; and the second stone in carn W is a similar rock.

In the rear of the sixth or adjoining chamber there is placed a stone the necessity for which in the construction does not appear, as there is an upright behind it forming the back of the compartment. It is a diamond-shaped slab, one corner of which comes into view in the foregoing illustration, placed erect on one of its angles ; and it is not a little remarkable that the stone abutting on it is elaborately carved on both sides with diamond-shaped figures. A Celtic drinking cup, with handle, was discovered by Mr. Bateman in 1850, in a carn about a mile north of Pickering, which was found to be decorated with this same diamond-shaped pattern. Of it he says :—" The ornamentation of the vessel is peculiar, consisting chiefly of angularly-pointed cartouches, filled with a reticulated pattern, and having a band of the same encircling the upper part."

Eighteen of the stones in this carn are inscribed.

M.

About 650 yards to the S. E. of L, and crowning the next knoll, called Carrickbrac, from the speckled nature of the rock which forms the hill, are the remains of a carn twenty-two yards in diameter, at present only about four feet high, and wanting the usual boundary ring of large stones as well as internal chambers.

N.

On the top of a second knoll, 572 yards due east from M, are the *debris* of a carn, twenty-two yards in diameter. At present not more than two feet in height of the small stones which composed it remain. Four large stones outside this carn mark an avenue pointing due east, of sixteen yards long, seven yards wide at the entrance, and diminishing to four yards wide as it approaches the carn. One of these stones standing upwards of six feet above the surface of the ground is inscribed with forty-eight cup-hollows.

O.

In the valley below the two knolls, 352 yards N. E. from M, and 279 yards N. W. from N, are the remains of a carn eleven yards in diameter. Three large prostrate stones, each measuring about 4 × 3 feet, mark the site. One upright stone, three feet nine inches high, three feet nine inches broad, and about one foot thick, is still standing, apparently in the circumference of the original carn. On its western face, arranged principally in four groups, are thirty-nine cups varying from half to three-quarters of an inch in diameter, and about a quarter of an inch deep.

P¹.

143 yards N. E. from N. are the remains of a carn, eight yards in diameter. Sufficient stones only remain to denote the original basis of the carn.

P².

About twenty-two yards northwards are six large stones, probably the remains of another carn.

---

* See Bateman's " Ten Years' Diggings," p. 209.

I

Q.

Thirty-eight yards northward from P² are the remains of another carn, four and a half yards in diameter. Nearly all the stones which composed it have been carried away.

R¹.

Passing up the hill in an easterly direction, and at a distance of 242 yards from Q, we come to the remains of a carn, eleven yards in diameter. All that now remains of the original pile varies from two to three feet in height.

R².

Sixteen yards to the south of R¹, and fifty-five yards S. W. from T, are the remains of another carn, nine yards in diameter, and about two feet in height. Ten of the stones forming its circular boundary still remain ; and outside the carn, at a distance of from three to four yards, lie five large stones.

S.

S is only five yards to the west of T, and fifty-one yards from R¹. Thirty-three large stones standing on ends form a circle, eighteen and a half yards in dia-meter, round the present remains. The apex of this carn is completely gone, leaving exposed the tops of the upright stones forming the chambers, the ar-rangement of which here differs from the others in having the passage or en-trance from the west—exact bearing W. 10° N. The entire length of the passage and chambers taken together is fifteen feet. The passage itself, which varies in breadth from two feet three inches to two feet seven inches, is divided by transverse upright stones into two compartments, each about two feet square. Immediately outside the entrance of the passage was found a perfect specimen of a leaf-shaped arrow-head, in white flint, an inch and a half long, and nearly three-quarters of an inch broad. Dr. Thurnam, who has seen it, pronounces it to be somewhat larger than those of the same unbarbed type found by him in the Wiltshire barrows. The two small compartments into which the pas-sage itself is divided were filled up to the height of eighteen inches with charred bones, broken into small fragments. On the top of these, in the first chamber, a piece of bent bone, tooled and rounded at one end, and nine inches in length, was found to be silicified. In the second chamber, and also on the top of the charred bones which filled the compartment, a roughly finished bone dagger was found, seven inches long and nearly an inch broad at the extremity of the handle, its widest part. Nearly covering the entire floor in each compartment rested a thin flag, underneath which were found splinters of burned bones, intermixed with small stones and pieces of charcoal.

Six of the chamber stones here are inscribed.

T.

Described under the head of Ollamh Fodhla's tomb.

U.

U is situated fourteen yards N. E. from T, and forty-six yards east of S. There are sixteen large stones still in the base ; and nearly two feet inside the circumference, a stone measuring eight feet two inches long, two feet four inches broad, and one foot eight inches thick, lies opposite the commencement of the passage. The present remains are only from four to five feet high, and fourteen and a half yards in diameter. The tops of the upright stones were left visible, and the chambers themselves more than half filled up with loose stones and earth. On removing these, the interior arrangement of the chambers was found, as in most other cases, to be cruciform. The length of the passage alone, which has a bearing of E. 20° S., is nine feet; and from the commencement of the passage to the extremity of the opposite chamber is twenty feet; while the breadth across the chambers is ten feet. One of the chamber stones is wanting, and another is displaced. When the stones which filled up these chambers were removed, the earth at the bottom, in some places from twelve to eighteen inches in depth, was found to be thickly mixed with splinters of burned bones.

We were informed by an old herd on the mountain that he recollected the chambers in this carn, in their half-cleared-out state, to have been used for culinary purposes by the men of the Ordnance Survey, when encamped on Sliabh na Caillighe in 1836.

There are fourteen inscribed stones in this carn.

There are some appearances of a carn having stood about midway between U and V.

V.

V is thirty-nine yards south-east from T, fifty-one yards south of U, and is eleven yards in diameter. All the smaller stones which originally formed the carn have been carried away, leaving quite bare the upright stones constituting the interior chambers. From present appearances these do not seem to have been arranged on any particular plan. The greatest length of the chambers, having a bearing of E. 20° S., is twenty-one feet, and breadth ten feet. About a yard outside the circumference, on the north-western side, stands an upright pillar stone, five feet above ground, five feet six inches broad, and one foot six inches thick. Digging round the base of this stone, in a fruitless search for inscriptions, we turned up a long, rounded, white sea pebble, which, from appearances, may have been used as a sling stone or a hammer.

Four of the upright stones in this carn are inscribed.

W.

W is 128 yards east of T. Its present remains appear nearly level with the ground, and are seven yards in diameter. The single interior chamber which this carn contained is round, or well-shaped; and unlike all the others, which appear to have been erected on the bare surface of the ground, the earth seems to have been dug away for the construction of this chamber, six feet nine inches in diameter, formed by eight flagstones placed on ends, fitting closely together, except in two instances, and all having an inclination inwards at the bottom. A layer of charred bones, six inches in thickness, was found to cover the bottom of this chamber; in the clearing out of which was brought to light, resting on the floor, a rude stone urn, hollowed on top to a depth of four and a half inches, one foot in height, and two feet eleven inches long by two feet six inches wide. On raising this urn, which evidently occupied its original position near the centre of the carn, some splinters of charred bones were found beneath it. The point which appears to have been the entrance to this chamber has a bearing due south.

Five of the chamber stones in this carn are inscribed.

About midway down the hill in a north-easterly direction is a large rock, nearly ten feet in length, now lying split into three parts, upon the upper surface of which is engraved a large star of eight rays, above which two straight lines are found crossing each other, and a sloped line higher up on the stone. A few yards further down, at the base of the hill, are the shattered remains of some great primitive monument. The upper surface of the now recumbent and uppermost rock, which appears to have fallen southwards, contains fifty cup-hollows, which have been apparently *ground* into the stone. About 120 yards north of this point are two earth-fast monuments. One leaning towards the east has split with the lamination of the rock into three parts. It is about four feet six inches over ground, and contains thirty-three cup-hollows ground into its surface. The other is a natural rock, cropping up with an angle of about 30° towards the south, the exposed surface, being about eight feet in slant height, and having ninety cup-hollows ground into it ; besides two cups, each surrounded by a circle. A short distance north of these two monuments, on the flat open plain, but unfortunately intersected by a dry stone ditch, are the remains of the stone circle of Ballinvalley, about twenty-five yards in diameter, consisting of seven stones, some still erect, and averaging about seven feet in height, the highest being eight feet two inches over ground.

X.

Passing from the hill specially known as Sliabh na Caillighe, and midway up the next or eastern peak, called the Hill of Patrickstown, are found together the remains of three stone circles. The northern circle is the most perfect of the three, the other two being in their present state little more than semicircles. The diameter of this circle is forty feet. Commencing with the most northern stone, and proceeding in a south-westerly direction, the distance from stone No. 1 to No. 2 is four yards ; from 2 to 3, four yards ; from 3 to 4, one yard ; 4 and 5 nearly touch one another ; distance from 5 to 6, two yards ; 6 and 7 nearly touch one another ; distance from 7 to 8, three yards ; from 8 to 9 eight yards ; and from 9 to 1 twelve yards.

Thirteen feet inwards from the circumference stands an upright stone, upon the face of which, pointing N. W., are inscribed a very remarkable grouping of cups, circles, and star-like figures, which can be only seen to advantage in a suitable shade of sunlight.

The middle circle is nine yards south of the northern circle, and is twelve yards in diameter. The distance from stone No. 1 to No. 2 is four yards ; from 2 to 3, one yard ; from 3 to 4, two yards ; from 4 to 5, two yards ; from 5 to 6, three yards. No. 5 is inscribed with a cup, having ten others in a circle round it ; the circle measuring ten inches across, and having four other cups in an incomplete circle round this again, nearly eighteen inches across, the cups being about an inch and a half in diameter and a quarter of an inch deep ; there are also twenty-eight similar cups in one group on this stone. In the centre of the circle are lying flat two stones, one of which contains a circular hole, six and a half inches in diameter, cut vertically, with much precision and smoothness, to a depth of three inches. For what use this may have been intended was long a puzzle to us, until at length we learned that in 1836, the sappers had made and used it for the insertion of a flag-staff.

The third, or southern circle, twelve yards south of the middle one, and twenty-three yards in diameter, at present contains only seven stones, with an eighth lying five yards west of its boundary. The distance from No. 1 to No. 2 is seven yards ; from 2 to 3, fifteen yards ; from 3 to 4, four yards ;

from 4 to 5, nine yards; and Nos. 5, 6, and 7 adjoin one another. Upon a stone in the adjoining fence opposite the south circle is inscribed a cup surrounded by a circle ; and higher up upon the stone are nine single cups.

Y.

Crowning the top of the Hill of Patrickstown, which attains the height of 885 feet, there stood until within the past few years one of the most conspicuous carns in the range.* The diameter of its site is thirty-three yards ; but only a few cartloads of the stones which formed it now remain, the rest having been used up by the proprietor of the hill, in the construction of adjoining fences.†

Z.

At the base of the eastern peak, on the south side, stands the Moat of Patrickstown. ' It measures 115 paces round the base, forty-five feet in slant height, and forty paces round the circumference at the top, which is flattened. This tumulus is situated on the top of a small sloping eminence in a green field, and is crowned by a mutilated whitethorn tree, growing on its eastern border. It is covered with earth and grass, but it is said to contain stone chambers in the interior.

At what remote, or even recent period, these ancient tombs have been subjected to demolition, it would be difficult to determine. We have heard, however, from old men who were engaged at the work of exploration, that they recollected, before quarries were generally opened in the country, that persons were in the habit of coming from distances of twenty and thirty miles round about, to procure from these archaic structures slabs suitable for domestic or other purposes, and, in this way, it is probable that many, if not all, the missing roofing stones of the passages and chambers have disappeared.

It is a remarkable fact that, although the inscribed stones still remaining in these carns exceed 100 in number, there are not two the designs on which are similar.

On the stones which have been long exposed to the destructive effects of the atmosphere, the punched or other work is often much obliterated ; but on those brought to light in 1865, the work of the tool was almost as fresh and as distinct as at the period of its execution.

---

* See p. 23.

† Nearly four hundred yards east of this carn are the remains of a burying place, measuring 16 × 14 yards in extent, and raised three or four feet higher than the adjoining ground. Early in the sixteenth century a regular battle was fought on this hill between two neighbouring septs—the Plunkets and the O'Reillys ; and it is said that the dead of both parties who remained on the field after the battle were interred here. The inclosure contains an upright stone—possibly the shaft of a rude cross—measuring seven feet in height, one foot six inches broad, and eight inches thick. Near the gate opening out upon the road which here crosses the Hill of Patrickstown a few stones are placed together in the form of a square. There is a tradition in the neighbourhood that a man and his wife are buried here, who, to avoid taking any part in the above battle, fled to the town of Kells until the fight was over; but, on their return, they were met on the very site of the contest and put to death.

CORRIGENDA.